CREEPY CRAWLY CROCHET

17 Creatures That Go Bump in the Night

Megan Kreiner

DOVER PUBLICATIONS

Garden City, New York

Creature photography: Tommy Muller

Step-by-Step

Model and crocheter: Pat Olski
Photography: Cynthia Castellari and Charles Young

Bibliographical Note

*Creepy Crawly Crochet: 17 Creatures That Go
Bump in the Night* is a new work,
first published by Dover Publications
in 2016. The author is represented by
MacGregor Literary, Inc.

*Library of Congress
Cataloging-in-Publication Data*

Names: Kreiner, Megan, 1981–author.
Title: Creepy crawly crochet : 17 creatures that go
    bump in the night / Megan Kreiner.
Description: Garden City, New York : Dover
    Publications [2016]
Identifiers: LCCN 2016020924 | ISBN 9780486810799
    | ISBN 0486810798
Subjects: LCSH: Crocheting—Patterns. | Monsters
    in art.
Classification: LCC TT829 .K74 2016
    | DDC 746.43/4—dc23 LC record available at
    https://lccn.loc.gov/2016020924

Manufactured in the United States of America
81079805
www.doverpublications.com

CONTENTS

DEDICATION

To my two favorite monsters, James and Emily.

INTRODUCTION

It was a dark and stormy night. By the light of a dim lamp, she sat alone, quietly crocheting. Then, with only three more rows to go, her last skein of yarn suddenly RAN OUT!!!

AAAAHHHH!!!!!!!

Now that you've been properly horrified, prepare to be scared silly by seventeen of the creepiest (and yet somewhat adorable) crochet creature patterns you've ever seen! Bring your very own Frankenstein's monster to life as well as his blushing bride (who now runs Dr. Frankenstein's lab after the doctor met with a rather unfortunate . . . accident).

Scare your friends with an adorable army of roly-poly voodoo dolls. Frighten off your coworkers with an evil bunny for your desk. Shake in terror at the idea of having to crochet eight spider legs. (It's totally worth it though . . . she's a very cute spider!)

I hope you'll enjoy all the shrieks (of joy) these creepy toys are sure to elicit from friends, family, and fleeing coworkers.

Happy Crocheting!

—Megan Kreiner of MK Crochet

mk crochet ®

GETTING STARTED

MATERIALS

Before you begin your first creature creation, check over your materials to make sure you have everything you need to get started!

Yarn: When it comes to making toys, think quality over quantity. Since all of the patterns require a skein or less of each yarn color, try to choose yarns that will crochet into a smooth and sturdy material. Good quality cotton, blended fibers, and acrylic yarns hold up fairly well when made into toys.

Refer to the Pattern Yarns section on page 106 for a complete listing of the yarns used for each project in this book.

Felt: Many of the patterns in this book have finishing details such as eyes or fangs that are created using felt patches. Good quality felt can make the difference between a fuzzy mess and a crisp, clean-looking felt patch. It's worth the splurge to get the good stuff. When tracing shapes onto your felt, white gel pens work well on dark-colored felts and ballpoint pens or pencils work well on light-colored felts.

Stuffing: For easy cleaning and care, polyester fiberfill stuffing is readily available at most craft stores and will maintain its shape over time.

For dark-colored toys, white stuffing can sometimes show through, even when your gauge is fairly tight. Black stuffing can be tricky to locate, but around October, you may come across a product called "Halloween Hay" from Polyester Fibers at your local craft store, which is essentially black polyester fiberfill. This stuff is great for dark-colored toys, so if you find it, consider stocking up!

NOTIONS & TOOLS

A complete arsenal of tools and notions will help make the process of bringing your monsters to life quick and nearly painless!

Crochet Hook: There are lots of options in regard to materials and handle styles for crochet hooks. I prefer metal hooks with ergonomic handles since they won't bend easily. If possible, hold the hook in your hand before you make your purchase to ensure a comfortable fit.

The suggested hook size for the patterns in this book is a size F (3.75 mm) crochet hook. However, because you're making toys and not garments, your stitch gauge and overall sizing is not crucial. Just be sure your stitches are tight enough so your stuffing doesn't show through, and resize your felt patches accordingly.

Scissors: Fabric scissors used exclusively for yarn will help ensure clean cuts and quick snips. A small pair of cuticle scissors can also be helpful and more accurate when cutting out small felt patches.

Tapestry Needles: A few steel tapestry needles will make assembling your creepy creatures a snap. Avoid plastic tapestry needles since they can sometimes bend and break when going through thick materials like felt or a tightly stuffed toy.

Craft Glue: My preferred method of attaching patches is to use a thick craft glue (such as Sobo or Aleene's) that won't soak into the yarn fibers right away.

Split Rings: Use these rings for when a pattern calls for a "place marker" (pm) to help mark useful landmarks on your work. This kind of a marking ring can also help you track where your round begins, and will hold two edges of your work together for easier sewing.

Stitch Counter: A small counter can help you keep track of where you are in your pattern.

Marking Pins: Pins with round plastic or glass heads are a big help when working out how to assemble your finished pieces so your completed toy will be evenly constructed.

Project Bags: A small project bag (such as a pencil case) is great for storing smaller tools and notions, while a larger bag can hold everything you need for your current project.

CROCHET STITCHES

If you are new to crocheting, this section will provide an overview of all the stitches used for the patterns in this book.

SLIPKNOT

1. Make a loop with a 6in/15.25cm tail. Overlap the loop on top of the working yarn coming out of the skein.

2. Slip your hook into the loop and under the working yarn and gently pull to tighten the yarn around the hook.

YARN OVER (YO)

Wrap the yarn over your hook from back to front.

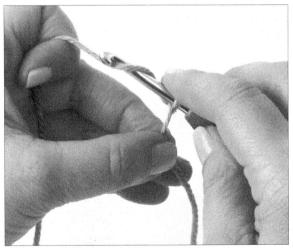

CHAIN (ch)

1. Make a slipknot on your hook.
2. Yarn over (YO) and draw the yarn through the loop on your hook. You will now have a new loop on your hook with a slipknot below it.

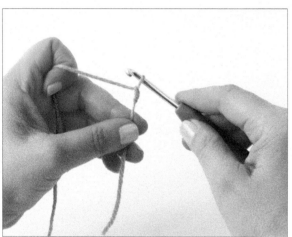

3. Repeat Step 2 until you've reached the specified number of chain stitches. When counting, only the chains below the loop on the hook should be counted.

SLIP STITCH (sl st)

1. Insert your hook into the next chain or stitch.

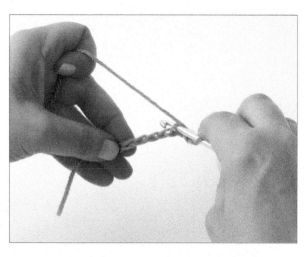

2. While keeping your tension as loose as possible, YO and draw the yarn through the stitch and the loop on your hook.

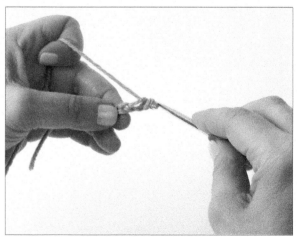

SINGLE CROCHET (sc)

1. Insert your hook into a chain or stitch and YO. Draw the yarn through the chain or stitch. You will have two loops on your hook.

2. YO and draw yarn through both loops on your hook to complete the single crochet.

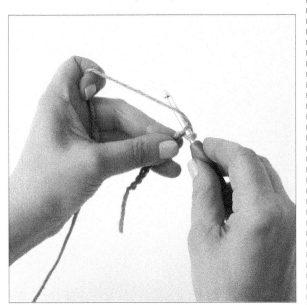

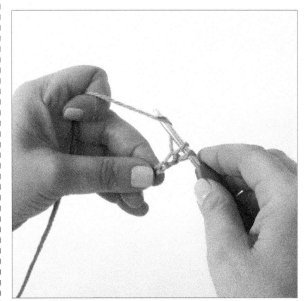

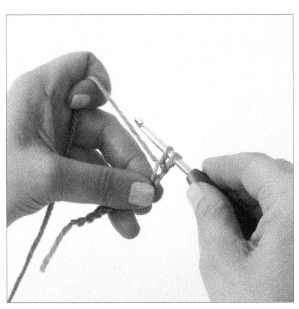

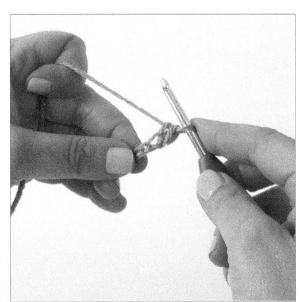

HALF DOUBLE CROCHET (hdc)

1. YO and insert your hook into a chain or stitch. YO a second time and draw the yarn through the chain or stitch. You will have three loops on your hook.

2. YO and draw yarn through all three loops on your hook to complete the half double crochet.

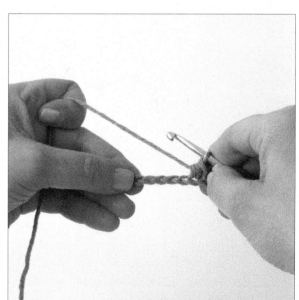

DOUBLE CROCHET (dc)

1. YO and insert your hook into a chain or stitch. YO a second time and draw the yarn through the chain or stitch. You will have three loops on your hook.

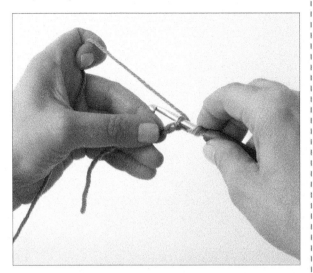

2. YO and draw yarn through just the first two loops on your hook. You will have two loops remaining on your hook.

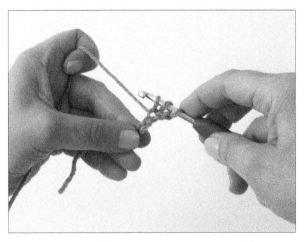

3. YO and draw yarn through the last two loops on your hook to complete the double crochet.

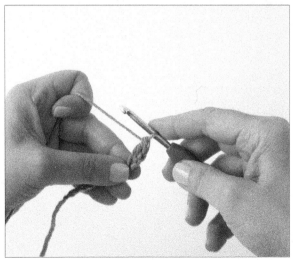

TRIPLE CROCHET (tr)

1. YO two times and insert your hook into a chain or stitch. YO a third time and draw the yarn through the chain or stitch. You will have four loops on your hook.

2. YO and draw yarn through the first two loops on your hook. You will have three loops remaining on your hook.

3. YO and draw yarn through the next two loops on your hook. You will have two loops remaining on your hook.

4. YO and draw yarn through the remaining two loops on your hook to finish the triple crochet.

FRONT POST STITCH (Shown as Front Post Double Crochet—FPdc)

1. YO and insert your hook below your next stitch to the right of your stitch's post. Work the hook around the post from front to back to front again. YO and draw yarn through. You will have three loops on your hook.

2. YO and draw yarn through just the first two loops on your hook. You will have two loops remaining on your hook. YO and draw yarn through the last two loops on your hook to complete the double crochet.

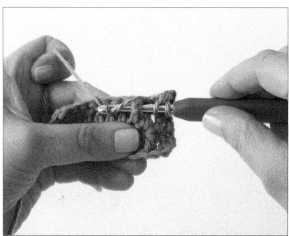

BACK POST STITCH (Shown as Back Post Double Crochet—BPdc)

1. YO and insert your hook behind and below your next stitch to the right of your stitch's post. Work the hook around the post from back to front to back again and YO.

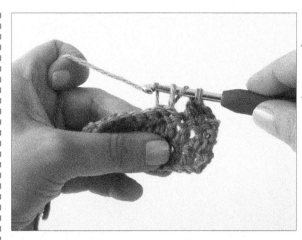

You can also work around the post in the same way using other stitches such as sc (FPsc) and hdc (FPhdc / BPhdc).

2. YO and draw yarn through just the first two loops on your hook. You will have two loops remaining on your hook. YO and draw yarn through the last two loops on your hook to complete the double crochet.

INCREASES (Sc 2 in next st)
Work two or more stitches into the same stitch when indicated.

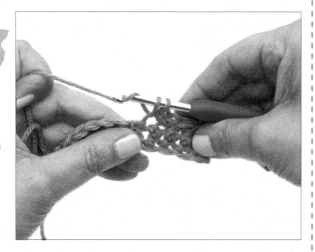

DECREASES
There are two kinds of decreases used in this book's patterns: Single Crochet Decreases and Skipped Stitches.

Single Crochet 2 together (Sc2tog)
1. Insert your hook into the next stitch, YO and draw the yarn through the stitch. You will have two loops on your hook.

2. Repeat Step 1 in following stitch. You will have three loops on your hook.

3. YO and draw yarn through all three loops on your hook to finish the decrease.

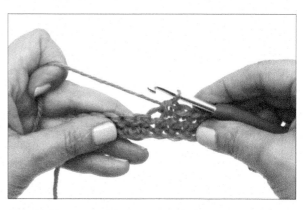

Skip (sk)
Per the pattern instructions, count and skip the number of stitches indicated before working the next stitch in the pattern.

WORKING IN BACK LOOPS ONLY (blo) and Front Loops Only (flo)
For all patterns, work in both loops of a stitch except when the pattern instructs that a stitch should be worked in the back loop or front loop. The front loop is the loop closest to you. The back loop is behind the front loop. If a round or row begins with "In blo" or "In flo" work entire rnd/row in that manner unless you are instructed to switch.

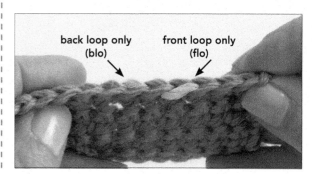

back loop only (blo)   front loop only (flo)

CROCHET TECHNIQUES

WORKING IN THE ROUND

Many patterns in this book are worked in a spiral round in which there are no slip stitches or chains between rounds. Just keep crocheting from one round to the next. If needed, use stitch markers to keep track of where your rounds begin and end.

ADJUSTABLE RING (AR)

The adjustable ring is a great technique that will minimize the hole that commonly appears in the middle of a starting round.

1. Form a ring with your yarn, leaving a 6in/15.25cm tail. Insert the hook into the loop as if you were making a slipknot.

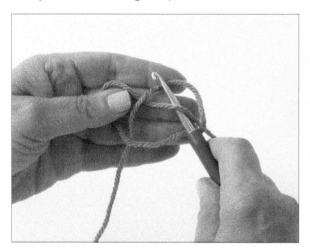

2. YO the hook and pull through the loop to make a slip stitch but do not tighten the loop.

3. Ch 1 and then sc over both strands of yarn that make up the edge of the adjustable ring until you've reached the number of stitches indicated in the pattern. To close the center of the ring, pull firmly on the yarn tail.

To start your next round, work your next stitch in the first single crochet of the completed adjustable ring. If the pattern requires a semi-circle shape (like for an ear), ch 1 and turn the work so that the back of the piece faces you before working the next row in your pattern.

WORKING AROUND A CHAIN

When working around a chain of stitches, you'll first work in the back ridge loops of the chain and then in the front loops of the chain to create your first round.

1. Make a chain per the pattern instructions. To begin round 1, work your first stitch in the back ridge loop of the second chain from your hook (feel free to mark this stitch with a stitch marker to make it easy to find). Work the rest of your stitches into the back ridge loops of the chain until you've reached the last chain above the slipknot. Work the indicated number of stitches into the back ridge loop of this last chain.

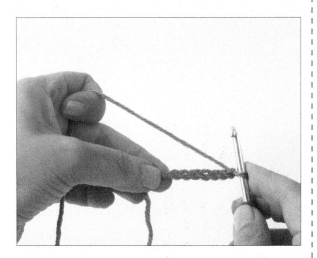

2. When you're ready to work the other side of the chain, rotate your work so the front loops of the chain face up. Starting in the next chain, insert your hook under the two front loops of the chain to work your next stitch.

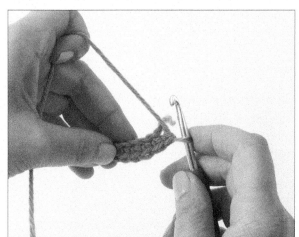

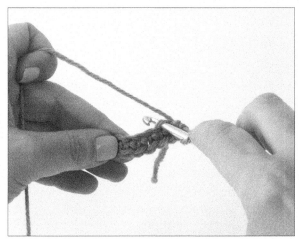

3. Once you have finished working the rest of the stitches into the front loops of round 1, continue on to round 2 (indicated by your stitch marker).

RIGHT SIDE (RS) / WRONG SIDE (WS)

When working in the round, the side of your pattern perceived as the "right side" will affect which part of the stitch is the back loop versus the front loop. As a general rule, the 6in/15.25cm tail left over from forming the adjustable ring will usually lie on the wrong side (WS) of the piece. The same can be said for patterns that begin by working around a chain provided you hold the 6in/15.25cm yarn tail at the back of your work as you crochet the 1st round.

CHANGING COLORS

Work the stitch prior to the color change right up to the last step in which you would normally draw the yarn through the loop(s) on your hook to complete the stitch.

To change colors, YO the hook with your new color and draw the new color through the remaining loop(s) on your hook, completing the stitch. You can then continue on to the next stitch in the new color.

For color changes at the beginning of a new row, complete the stitch in your previous row, then introduce the new color when you ch 1 and turn. Continue to work with your new color for the next row.

For color changes that take place in a slip stitch, simply insert the hook into the old color stitch, YO with the new color, and draw the new color through the loop on your hook to complete your slip stitch and the color change.

CROCHETING ON THE SURFACE

Add additional details to your work by crocheting onto the surface of your pieces. This technique can be worked in any surface stitch or in the raised loops that will be visible after you've worked a round in the back loops of your stitches or in the front posts.

1. Draw a loop of yarn through the surface of your work.

2. Ch 1 and apply a stitch (such as a slip stitch) into the same surface loop you started in. This will create your first surface stitch.

You can then continue to work in a specific set of stitches or apply a line of free-form surface stitches to your piece.

FINISHING TOUCHES

Assemble and customize your creations with a few simple sewing and embroidery stitches. Your creatures will be put together in no time (except, perhaps, for Zombie Dog, since he's rocking that falling-apart look).

WHIPSTITCH

Use this stitch to close seams and attach open edges on your work. Using your tapestry needle and yarn, draw your needle and yarn through your work and catch the edge(s) of the second piece you wish to sew in place. Pull the yarn through the edge(s) before drawing the yarn through your work again in a spiral-like motion. Continue until the seam is closed or the piece is attached.

MATTRESS STITCH

The mattress stitch will give you a nice tight seam between various creature pieces, such as for sewing down the open edges of tails and muzzles, and for joining crocheted heads and bodies together.

Select a point on the surface or edge of your first piece and insert the needle from A to B and pull the yarn through. Cross over to the surface of your second piece and draw your needle in and out from C to D with the entry point at C lining up between points A and B on the first surface. Return to the first surface and insert your needle directly next to exit point B. Continue to work back and forth in this manner until the seam is closed, pulling firmly after every few stitches to ensure a clean, tight seam.

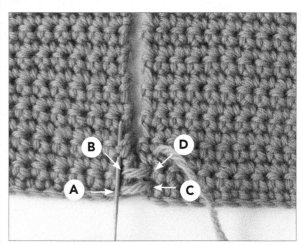

Pro Tip!

Leave long yarn tails when you fasten off your arms and legs. When assembling, use straight pins to attach all your limbs to the body to ensure everything is even and balanced. Then, using the leftover yarn tails, place a single stitch at each straight pin to tack your pieces in place. Remove the pins and finish sewing your pieces down using a whip or mattress stitch.

SHORT / LONG STITCHES

Shape the surface of your character, such as the toes or fingers, with short and long stitches. With your yarn and a metal tapestry needle, draw the yarn up through the surface of your piece (A) and then reinsert the needle in a different location (B). Repeat if desired to double or triple up the yarn. To cinch the surface of your piece, pull the yarn firmly as you work.

SATIN STITCH

Apply satin stitches by grouping short- or medium-length stitches closely together to build up a shape or to fill in an area with color.

RUNNING STITCH

Attach felt pieces or flattened crochet pieces to your work with thread (instead of glue) by using a running stitch. Run your needle in and out of the surface of your piece in a dashed-line pattern.

BACK STITCH

Use this stitch to create solid line details on the surface of your work. Begin by drawing the yarn up through the surface of your piece. Reinsert the needle to the right, then bring it up slightly to the left of the first stitch as shown. Continue to work in this manner to make a solid line of stitches.

LAZY DAISY STITCH

This stitch can be adjusted to create tight petal shapes or wide eyebrow shapes. Begin by drawing the yarn up through the surface of your piece and then reinsert the needle in the same place, leaving the yarn loose to achieve the desired level of curve. Choose a point along the curved long stitch and draw up the yarn inside of the curve and reinsert on other side of yarn as shown to hold the shape of the long stitch in place. Feel free to repeat if desired at other points along the long stitch if needed.

CHAIN STITCH

Bring your needle up into the work and reinsert it in the same place and bring it out a short distance away inside the loop as if to make a lazy daisy stitch. Reinsert the needle into the same place and continue in this manner as shown.

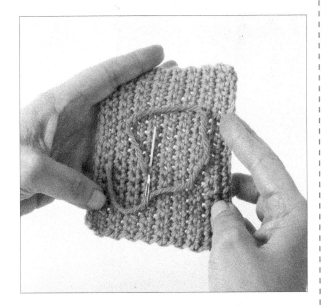

Bring your needle up through your work a stitch below your last chain. Slide the needle under your last chain, and reinsert the needle into its starting point. Repeat.

FRENCH KNOT

With the yarn and needle on the right side of the work, hold the yarn close to the surface of the work where the yarn has most recently emerged. Wind the yarn around the needle (you can wind it two times if you would like to make a larger knot). While applying tension to the yarn, insert the needle close to where the yarn most recently emerged. Pull the needle through the work, leaving a knot on the surface.

CHUNKY FRENCH KNOT

To bulk up the French knot, draw the needle and yarn out at the base of the completed French knot and proceed to wind the yarn around the base of the French knot three or four times. To secure, draw the needle through the top surface of the French knot to catch a few loops and pull tightly.

FRINGE TECHNIQUE

Insert your hook through a surface stitch on your work and fold a 4in/10.25cm piece of yarn over the hook. Draw the folded yarn through the surface stitch to create a loop on your hook. Bring the yarn tails through this loop and pull tightly to secure it.

Use the fringe technique to apply strands of yarn to the surface of your work in a cluster to cover the area where you wish to add fringe. Once you are happy with the coverage, use your tapestry needle to separate the yarn plies. Use your fingers or a fine tooth comb to make the fringe even more soft and frizzled. Trim to the desired length.

TIPS & TRICKS

Add a bit of spooky flare to your creatures with hidden magnets, movable button joints, posable bones, and twisted whiskers.

SEW IN EARTH MAGNETS
Create a little monster magic by installing earth magnets so Jack the Headless Horseman will stay firmly in his saddle.

You will need:
2 earth magnets
Four 3in/7.50cm squares of cotton fabric
Fabric glue or needle and thread

Place one magnet in the center of one 3in/7.50cm square of fabric. Spread fabric glue onto the square around the magnet and place the other fabric square on top, sandwiching the magnet in between the two layers of fabric. Allow the glue to dry and trim the excess material around the magnet to about ¼in/.75cm border. Repeat on the second magnet.

SHANK BUTTON JOINTS
Create movable pivot points at the hips and shoulders of your creature by using shank-style buttons.

You will need:
½in/1.25cm plastic shank buttons for each joint
Felt (for larger pieces)
Tapestry needle

Begin by threading a 12–16in/30.50–40.50cm strand of yarn through the hole in the back of the button and tie the yarn off, leaving two 6–8in/15.25–20.25cm tails.

If the pivot joint will be for a larger piece (such as a neck joint), cut a 1in/2.50cm circle of felt out and make a small hole in the center of the felt circle. Draw the yarn tails through the hole before installing the shank button. The felt circle will act as a washer.

To install, place both yarn tails onto a tapestry needle. Starting on the inside of your piece, draw the yarn tails out through the surface of your work. Tuck the button (and felt circle if needed) into position on the inside of your piece. Add stuffing, if needed, before closing up the seams.

To ensure a snug fit, draw the yarn tails through the body with a tapestry needle to the opposite hip or shoulder, then secure and fasten off.

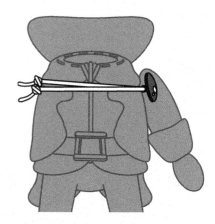

PIPE CLEANER SKELETON

To add a bit more rigidity to your character, you can add pipe cleaners to the legs or arms before attaching to the body to make your creature more posable and stable.

You will need:
Pipe cleaners
Cloth / Gaffers tape (in white or black).

Take a pipe cleaner and form it into a flattened loop slightly shorter than the length of the limb you want to make sturdy. Wrap a little cloth tape around the twist points to cover any pointy ends. For a longer limb, knot a piece of yarn to the end of the loop. With a tapestry needle, thread the yarn down from the top open edge out through the bottom of the limb. Pull the yarn and gently twist the pipe cleaner to work it down and into the limb.

Trim yarn once the pipe cleaner is in place. Add more stuffing where needed.

ADDING WHISKERS

Give your creature some durable whiskers with this simple technique.

You will need:
Yarn or embroidery thread in whisker color
Craft glue

Take a strand of yarn and separate the plies. Take a single ply and secure it either under the chin or where the head meets the neck if you haven't already attached the head using the fringe technique. You should have two ply tails of equal length.

Draw each ply tail up into your work and out at the point you wish to have a whisker. Repeat this process until you have the desired number of whiskers.

Once the plies are in place, trim them longer than the final length and apply some craft glue to your fingertips. Coat each ply in glue by rolling it between your fingers to stiffen and shape it. Allow the whisker to dry completely before trimming it to the final length.

IMPORTANT!
Always work in back ridge loops of chain
unless otherwise instructed.

GHOULISH GRACE

Poor little Grace, all blue in the face. If only she had been a bit more graceful, she may not have tripped and fallen head over heels into that well long ago.

SKILL LEVEL
—Beginner

Height: 7½in/19cm, not including hair

MATERIALS

- Red Heart® Soft® 5oz/141g, 256yds/234m (100% acrylic)—one each: #4614 Black (A), #4600 White (B), #9820 Mid Blue (C)
- F-5 (3.75mm) crochet hook
- White felt and light green (honeydew) felt [see page 103 for felt templates]
- Fabric glue
- Sewing needle and thread in black

HEAD

Rnd 1: With C, 6 sc in adjustable ring—6 sts.

Rnd 2: 2 sc in each st around—12 sts.

Rnd 3: [Sc in next st, 2 sc in next st] 6 times—18 sts.

Rnd 4: [Sc in next 2 sts, 2 sc in next st] 6 times—24 sts.

Rnds 5–6, 8, 10–11: Sc in each st around.

Rnd 7: [Sc in next 4 sts, sc2tog] 4 times—20 sts.

Rnd 9: [Sc in next 3 sts, sc2tog] 4 times—16 sts.

Rnd 12: [Sc in next 2 sts, sc2tog] 4 times—12 sts.

Rnd 13: Sc in each st around. Stuff head.

Rnd 14: [Sc in next st, sc2tog] 4 times—8 sts. Fasten off and close hole.

EYE BASES (make 2)

Rnd 1: With A, 6 sc in adjustable ring—6 sts.

Rnd 2: [Sc in next 2 sts, 2 sc in next st] 2 times—8 sts. Fasten off. Sew edges to front of head. With A, embroider eyebrows and a small frowny mouth.

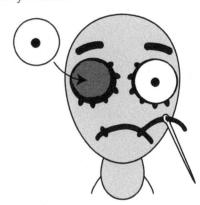

Cut two small circles from light green felt. Using black sewing thread, embroider a pupil on each eye. Glue or sew finished eyes to eye bases.

NOSE

With C, 4 sc in adjustable ring, sl st to join. Fasten off.

Use crochet hook handle to turn nose right side out. Sew open edge of nose to center of face.

EARS (make 2)

With C, 4 sc in adjustable ring. Do not join, tighten ring and fasten off pulling tail through 4th st. Sew straight edge to side of head.

BODY

Rnd 1: With B, 8 sc in adjustable ring—8 sts.

Rnd 2: 2 sc in each st around—16 sts.

Rnd 3: [Sc in next st, 2 sc in next st] 8 times—24 sts.

Rnd 4: [Sc in next 3 sts, 2 sc in next st] 6 times—30 sts.

Rnd 5: BPsc in each st around.

Rnds 6, 8–10, 12–15, 17–21: Sc in each st around.

Rnd 7: [Sc in next 4 sts, sc2tog] 5 times—25 sts.

Rnd 11: [Sc in next 3 sts, sc2tog] 5 times—20 sts.

Rnd 16: [Sc in next 2 sts, sc2tog] 5 times—15 sts.

Rnd 22: [Sc in next st, sc2tog] 5 times—10 sts. Stuff body.

Rnd 23: [Sc in next 3 sts, sc2tog] 2 times—8 sts.

Rnd 24: FPsc in each st around.

Rnd 25: With C, BLsc in each st around.

Rnd 26: Sc in each st around. Stuff neck. Fasten off. Sew open edge of neck to lower back of head.

DRESS RUFFLE

Rnd 1: With neck pointed down, working into top of Rnd 5, join B with (sl st, ch 1, sc) in any st, sc in next 29 sts—30 sts.

Rnd 2: 2 dc in each st around—60 sts.

Rnd 3: [Ch 2, hdc in next st] to last st, sc in last st. Fasten off. Work a running st bet Rnds 1 and 2 of ruffle and pull gently to gather skirt so body is sitting on the edge of Rnd 3.

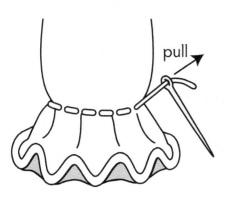

pull

HANDS AND ARMS (make 2)

Rnd 1: With C, 4 sc in adjustable ring—4 sts.

Rnd 2: 2 Sc in each st around—8 sts.

Rnds 3–4: Sc in each st around.

Rnd 5: [Sc in next 2 sts, sc2tog] 2 times—6 sts. Stuff hand.

Rnd 6: With B, FPsc in each st around.

Rnd 7: 2 Sc in each st around—12 sts.

Rnd 8: BPsc in each st around.

Rnd 9: [Sc in next st, sc2tog] 4 times—8 sts.

Rnd 10: [Sc in next 2 sts, sc2tog] 2 times—6 sts.

Rnds 11–14: Sc in each st around.

Fasten off. Stuff arm lightly, flatten seam at top of arm and sew closed.

CUFF

Rnd 1: With hand pointed up, working into FL on Rnd 8, (sl st, ch 1, sc) in any st to join B, Sc in next 11 sts—12 sts.

Rnd 2: Sc in each st around. Fasten off.

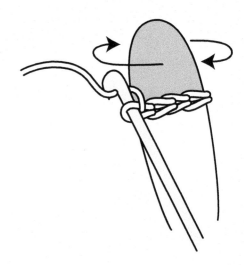

THUMBS (make 2)

Rnd 1: With C, 4 sc in adjustable ring—4 sts.

Rnd 2: Sc in each st around. Fasten off.

Use crochet hook handle to turn thumb right side out. Sew open edge of thumb to side of hand as illustrated. Sew finished arm to shoulder.

FINISHING

Cut 10 10–12in/25.5–30.5cm pieces of A and secure a line of fringe along the middle of the head (see page 21). Use a tapestry needle to separate yarn plies to give the hair a stringy look.

BUN BUN
OF THE DAMNED

Sure, he looks all cute and fluffy, but watch out for your fingers because, if you try to give him a scratch behind his ears, this little guy prefers thumbs over carrots!

SKILL LEVEL
—**Advanced Beginner**

Height: 7¾in/19.75cm, including ears

- - - - - - - - - - - - - - - - - - - -

MATERIALS

- Lion Brand Wool Ease® 3oz/85g, 197yds/180m (80% acrylic, 20% wool)—one each: #153 Black (A), #104 Blush Heather (B), #501 White Frost (C)
- F-5 (3.75mm) crochet hook
- White felt and red (poinsettia) felt [see page 103 for felt templates]
- Fabric glue
- Sewing needle and thread in white

HEAD

Rnd 1: With C, ch 9, sc in 2nd ch from hook and next 6 sts, 5 sc in next st. Rotate ch so front loops are facing up. Sc in next 6 sts, 4 sc in next st—22 sts.

Rnd 2: 2 hdc in next st, sc in next 6 sts, 2 hdc in next 5 sts, sc in next 6 sts, 2 hdc in next 4 sts—32 sts.

Rnd 3: 2 hdc in next 2 sts, sc in next 6 sts, 2 hdc in next 10 sts, sc in next 6 sts, 2 hdc in next 8 sts—52 sts.

Rnds 4–5: Sc in each st around.

Rnd 6: [Sc in next 11 sts, sc2tog] 4 times—48 sts.

Rnd 7: [Sc in next 4 sts, sc2tog] 8 times—40 sts.

Rnd 8: [Sc in next 8 sts, sc2tog] 4 times—36 sts.

Rnd 9: [Sc in next 4 sts, sc2tog] 6 times—30 sts.

Rnd 10: [Sc in next st, sc2tog] 10 times—20 sts.

Rnd 11: [Sc in next 3 sts, sc2tog] 4 times—16 sts. Stuff head.

Rnd 12: Sc2tog 8 times—8 sts. Fasten off, finish stuffing head and close hole.

EYES (make 2)

Rnd 1: With A, 8 sc in adjustable ring—8 sts.

Rnd 2: Sc in each st around.

Rnd 3: With C, 2 sc in each st around—16 sts.

Rnd 4: FPsc in each st around. Fasten off.

Sew eyes wide apart (about 10 sts bet) to front of head with a running st through Rnd 2. Using template, cut two pupils from red felt and 4 eye reflections from white felt. Glue or sew red pupils to black parts of eye, then glue or sew eye reflections to the red pupils as illustrated.

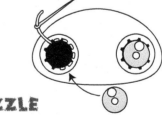

MUZZLE

Rnd 1: With C, ch 5, sc in 2nd ch from hook and in next 2 sts, 5 sc in next st. Rotate ch so front loops are facing up. Sc in next 2 sts, 4 sc in next st—14 sts.

Rnd 2: 2 sc in next st, sc in next 2 sts, 2 sc in next 2 sts, 2 hdc in next 3 sts, sc in next 2 sts, 2 hdc in next 3 sts, 2 sc in next st—24 sts.

Rnd 3: [Sc in next 2 sts, sc2tog] 6 times—18 sts.

Rnd 4: [Sc in next st, sc2tog] 6 times—12 sts. Fasten off.

With hdc sts in Rnd 2 facing down, sew open edge of muzzle to face bet eyes. Stuff and close seam. With C, gather the middle of the muzzle with 2–3 sts, pulling tightly to shape cheeks.

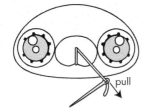

pull

NOSE

Row 1: With B, 3 sc in adjustable ring, turn—3 sts.

Row 2: Ch 1, sc in next st, 2 sc in next st, sc in next st, turn—4 sts.

Row 3: Ch 1, BLsc in each st across. Fasten off.

With front loops from row 3 facing out, sew nose above muzzle, stuff lightly if needed. With A, outline bottom of nose and lip cleft with long stitches in the shape of a "Y".

JAW

Rnd 1: With C, ch 4, sc in 2nd ch from hook and in next ch, 4 sc in next ch. Rotate ch so front loops are facing up. Sc in next 2 ch, 4 sc in next ch—12 sts.

Rnd 2: Sl st in next 4 sts, 2 sc in next 3 sts, sc in next st, 2 sc in next 3 sts, sl st in next st, turn.

Rnd 3: Ch 1, sc2tog 3 times, sc in next st, sc2tog 3 times, leave rem sts unworked. Fasten off.

Sew long flat edge of Rnd 3 to face directly under muzzle. Using templates, cut one inner mouth from red felt and two teeth from white felt. Glue or sew inner mouth to inside of jaw. Glue or sew teeth to inner mouth, tuck bases of teeth under cheeks.

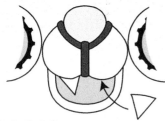

OUTER EARS (make 2)

Rnd 1: With C, ch 9, sc in 2nd ch from hook and in next 6 ch, 3 sc in next ch. Rotate ch so front loops are facing up. Sc in next 6 ch, 4 sc in next ch—20 sts.

Rnd 2: 2 sc in next st, sc in next 6 sts, 2 sc in next st, sc in next st, 2 sc in next st, sc in next 6 sts, 2 sc in next 4 sts—27 sts.

Rnds 3–4: Sc in each st around.

Rnd 5: Sc2tog, sc in next 6 sts, sc2tog, sc in next st, sc2tog, sc in next 6 sts, sc2tog 4 times—20 sts. Fasten off with tail at top of ear.

INNER EARS (make 2)

Rnd 1: With B, ch 9, sc in 2nd ch from hook and in next 6 ch, 3 sc in next ch. Rotate ch so front loops are facing up. Sc in next 6 ch, 4 sc in next ch—20 sts.

Rnd 2: 2 sc in next st, sc in next 6 sts, 2 sc in next st, sc in next st, 2 sc in next st, sc in next 6 sts, 2 sc in next 4 sts—27 sts. Fasten off with tail at top of ear.

With RS facing out, insert inner ear into outer ear. With C, whip st edges tog. With C, pinch bottom of ear tog and tack in place before securing ears to head. Attach 3–5 pieces of C to top of head for a fringe of hair (see page 21).

BODY

Rnd 1: With C, 10 sc in adjustable ring—10 sts.

Rnd 2: 2 sc in each st around—20 sts.

Rnd 3: [Sc in next st, 2 sc in next st] 10 times—30 sts.

Rnd 4: [Sc in next 2 sts, 2 sc in next st] 10 times—40 sts.

Rnds 5–6, 8, 10–12: Sc in each st around.

Rnd 7: [Sc in next 2 sts, sc2tog] 10 times—30 sts.

Rnd 9: [Sc in next st, sc2tog] 10 times—20 sts.

Rnd 13: [Sc in next 3 sts, sc2tog] 4 times—16 sts.

Rnds 14–15: Sc in each st around. Stuff body firmly.

Rnd 16: Sc2tog 8 times—8 sts. Fasten off.

Sew open edge of body to bottom of head. For bunny standing on all fours instead of upright, attach body to bottom of head, then tilt body back so it is parallel to the ground and sew the back of the lower head to the back of the upper body.

LEGS (make 2)

Rnd 1: With C, 8 sc in adjustable ring—8 sts.

Rnd 2: 2 sc in each st around—16 sts.

Rnd 3: [Sc in next st, 2 sc in next st] 8 times—24 sts.

Rnd 4: [Sc in next 3 sts, 2 sc in next st] 6 times—30 sts.

Rnd 5: [Sc in next 3 sts, sc2tog] 6 times—24 sts.

Rnd 6: [Sc in next st, sc2tog] 8 times—16 sts. Fasten off.

Sew open edges of legs to hips, lightly stuffing before closing seam.

FEET (make 2)

Rnd 1: With C, ch 4, sc in 2nd ch from hook and in next ch, 5 sc in next ch. Rotate ch so front loops are facing up. Sc in next ch, 4 sc in next ch—12 sts.

Rnd 2: [Sc in next 2 sts, 2 sc in next st] 4 times—16 sts.

Rnd 3: [Sc in next 3 sts, 2 sc in next st] 4 times—20 sts.

Rnd 4: Sc in each st around.

Rnd 5: [Sc in next 3 sts, sc2tog] 4 times—16 sts.

Rnd 6: [Sc in next 2 sts, sc2tog] 4 times—12 sts.

Rnds 7–11: Sc in each st around. Stuff foot.

Rnd 12: [Sc in next st, sc2tog] 4 times—8 sts.

Rnd 13: [Sc in next 2 sts, sc2tog] 2 times—6 sts. Fasten off and close hole in back of foot.

With larger end of foot facing forward, position back of foot under leg and edge of body, sew in place. With A, work 2 sets of long sts looped over front of foot. Pull tightly to separate toe shapes. Repeat on other foot.

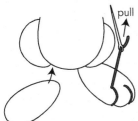

FRONT PAWS (make 2)

Rnd 1: With C, ch 4, sc in 2nd ch from hook and in next ch, 5 sc in next ch. Rotate ch so front loops are facing up. Sc in next ch, 4 sc in next ch—12 sts.

Rnd 2: [Sc in next 2 sts, 2 sc in next st] 4 times—16 sts.

Rnd 3: Sc in each st around.

Rnd 4: [Sc in next 2 sts, sc2tog] 4 times—12 sts.

Rnd 5: [Sc in next 4 sts, sc2tog] 2 times—10 sts.

Rnds 6–8: Sc in each st around. Stuff paw.

Rnd 9: [Sc in next 3 sts, sc2tog] 2 times—8 sts.

Rnd 10: [Sc in next 2 sts, sc2tog] 2 times—6 sts. Fasten off and close hole.

Sew tapered end of front paw to shoulder. With A, work 2 sets of long sts looped over front of paw. Pull tightly to separate toe shapes. Repeat on other front paw.

FINISHING

With C, make a pompom by winding yarn around a credit card 50–60 times. Tie off one side of the loops and cut the loops on the other side of the card. Fluff yarn with your fingers or with a brush and trim to desired size. Attach to back of bunny for tail.

Add whiskers if desired (see page 23).

POE THE RAVEN

Poe the Raven is judging you and your creative writing. He is not impressed!

SKILL LEVEL
—Advanced Beginner

Height: 6½ in/16.5cm, including feather fluff on head

- -

MATERIALS

- Red Heart® Soft® 5oz/141g, 256yds/234m (100% acrylic)—one each: #4614 Black (A), #9010 Charcoal (B)
- F-5 (3.75mm) crochet hook
- Gray (storm cloud) felt and black felt [see page 103 for felt templates]
- Black pipe cleaners (2)

BODY & HEAD

Rnd 1: With A, 8 sc in adjustable ring—8 sts.

Rnd 2: 2 sc in each st around—16 sts.

Rnd 3: [Sc in next 7 sts, 2 sc in next st] 2 times—18 sts.

Rnd 4: (tail opening) [Sc in next st, 2 sc in next st] 4 times, sc in next st, ch 6, sc in next st, [2 sc in next st, sc in next st] 4 times—32 sts.

Rnd 5: Sc in next 13 sts, sc in next 6 ch, sc in next 13 sts—32 sts.

Rnds 6–7, 9–11, 13, 17, 19, 21: Sc in each st around.

Rnd 8: [Sc in next 6 sts, sc2tog] 4 times—28 sts.

Rnds 12, 18: [Sc in next 5 sts, sc2tog] 4 times—24 sts.

Rnd 14: [Sc in next 2 sts, sc2tog] 6 times—18 sts.

Rnd 15: [Sc in next 2 sts, 2 sc in next st] 6 times—24 sts.

Rnd 16: [Sc in next 5 sts, 2 sc in next st] 4 times—28 sts.

Rnd 20: [Sc in next st, sc2tog] 8 times—16 sts.

Rnd 22: Sc2tog 8 times—8 sts. Fasten off and close hole. Stuff body and head firmly though tail opening.

TAIL

Rnd 1: Starting in lower right corner of tail opening, join A with (sl st, ch 1, sc) (counts as 1 sc), work 11 more sc around tail opening—12 sts.

Rnds 2–3: Sc in each st around.

Rnd 4: [Sc in next 2 sts, 2 sc in next st] 4 times—16 sts.

Rnd 5: [Sc in next st, 2 sc in next st] 8 times—24 sts.

Rnd 6: Sl st in next 12 sts, (sc, 2 hdc, sc) in next st, sl st in next 2 sts, (sc, hdc, ch 2, sl st in 2nd ch from hook, hdc, sc) in next st, sl st in next st, (sc, hdc, ch 3, sl st in 3rd ch from hook) in next st, (hdc, sc) in next st, sl st in next st, (sc, hdc, ch 2, sl st in 2nd ch from hook, hdc, sc) in next st, sl st in next 2 sts, (sc, 2 hdc, sc) in next st. Fasten off.

Add a small amount of stuffing to base of tail, flatten and sew opening closed (leaving the feathers loose)

Cut two 6in/15cm pieces of A and attach them through the top of the head to make a fringe. Separate the yarn plies and trim to desired length.

BEAK TOP

With B, ch 12, join with a sl st to form a ring, ch 1.

Rnds 1–4: Sc in each st around—12 sts.

Rnd 5: [Sc in next 2 sts, sc2tog] 3 times—9 sts.

Rnd 6: [Sc in next st, sc2tog] 3 times—6 sts.

Rnd 7: [Sc in next st, sc2tog] 2 times—4 sts. Fasten off and close hole at end of beak. Flatten back seam and sew tog.

BEAK BOTTOM

Rnd 1: With B, 4 sc in adjustable ring—4 sc.

Rnd 2: 2 sc in each st around—8 sts.

Rnd 3: BLsc in each st around.

Rnd 4: Sc in each st around.

Rnd 5: [Sc in next 2 sts, sc2tog] 2 times—6 sts.

Rnd 6: Sc in each st around. Fasten off, stuff and close hole.

Line up flat end of beak bottom with the flat seam of the beak top. Wrap edges of beak top around beak bottom and sew interior surfaces in place. Sew assembled beak to bottom half of head.

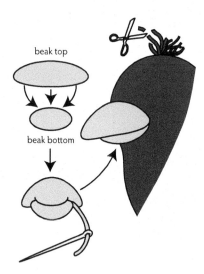

BEAK COVER

Row 1: With A, 6 sc in adjustable ring, turn—6 sts.

Row 2: Ch 1, sk 1, sl st in next 5 sts. Fasten off.

Sew beak cover on top of beak with flat edge against the head. With A, embroider a nostril on each side of beak. Create a mouth line by working a long st from one corner of the beak to the other, better defining the top and bottom. Work a few sts over mouth line to hold it in place if needed.

Cut two eyes from light grey felt and two pupils from black felt. Assemble eyes before gluing or sewing to face on either side of beak cover. With B, work 3–4 long satin stitches directly across top edge of eye for eyelids.

EYEBROWS (make 1)

Row 1: With A, ch 15, sl st in 2nd ch from hook, sc in next 5 ch, sl st in next 2 ch, sc in next 5 ch, sl st in next ch. Fasten off. Sew middle of eyebrow to back edge of beak cover. Shape brows into desired expression and sew in place above the eyes.

WINGS (make 2)

Rnd 1: With A, 6 sc in adjustable ring, turn—6 sts.

Rnd 2: Ch 1, 2 sc in each st around—12 sts.

Rnd 3: [Sc in next st, 2 sc in next st] 6 times—18 sts.

Rnd 4: [Sc in next 2 sts, 2 sc in next st] 6 times—24 sts.

Rnds 5, 7, 9, 11: Sc in each st around.

Rnd 6: [Sc in next 4 sts, sc2tog] 4 times—20 sts.

Rnd 8: [Sc in next 3 sts, sc2tog] 4 times—16 sts.

Rnd 10: [Sc in next 2 sts, sc2tog] 4 times—12 sts.

Rnd 12: [Sc in next st, sc2tog] 4 times—8 sts.

Rnd 13: [Sc in next 2 sts, sc2tog] 2 times—6 sts. Fasten off and close hole. Do not stuff.

Sew larger, rounder end of each wing to body at shoulder.

LEGS (make 2)

With A, ch 12, join with a sl st to form a ring, ch 1.

Rnd 1: Ch 1, sc in each st around—12 sts

Rnd 2: Sc in each st around—12 sts.

Rnd 3: [FPsc in next st, sk 1] 6 times—6 sts.

Rnd 4: With B, BLsc in each st around.

Rnds 5–7: Sc in each st around—6 sts.

Rnd 8: [Sc in next 2 sts, 2 sc in next st] 2 times—8 sts.

Rnd 9: *Sl st in next st, ch 6, working in back ridge loops hdc in 2nd ch from hook and in next 4 ch, sl st in st at base of ch**, sl st in next 2 sc, rep from *to** 3 times, sl st in next 2 sts. Fasten off.

FOOT BOTTOM (make 2)

Rnd 1: With B, 4 sc in adjustable ring—4 sts.

Rnd 2: 2 sc in each st around—8 sts.

Rnd 3: *Sl st in next st, ch 6, working in back ridge loops, hdc in 2nd ch from hook and in next 4 sts, sl st in st at base of ch**, sl st in next 2 sc, rep from *to** 3 times, sl st in next 2 sts. Fasten off.

Using foot bottom as a guide, with a black pipe cleaner make 4 flattened loops to fit within the 4 toes of the foot with the remaining pipe cleaner positioned straight up in the center for leg support. Fold over the tip of the pipe cleaner to blunt the end before inserting the straight section of the pipe cleaner into the leg. Match up the loops under the toes of the foot. With the RS of foot bottom facing out, match up toes with the toes from leg and whip st edges in place, encasing pipe cleaner. Stuff legs and base of legs before sewing open edges to the bottom of body.

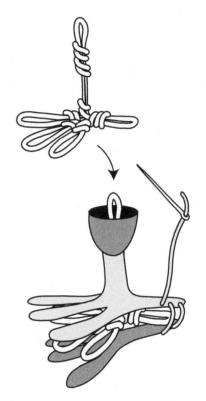

CLUMSY MUMSY

Poor Clumsy Mumsy is all wrapped up with no place to go. When a few miles of gauzy ribbon is your only wardrobe option, getting dressed in the morning can be an all-day affair.

SKILL LEVEL
— Advanced Beginner
Height: 9½ in/24.25cm

- - - - - - - - - - - - - - - - - - - -

MATERIALS

- Red Heart® Soft® 5oz/141g, 256yds/234m (100% acrylic)—one each: #1882 Toast (A), #4614 Black (B)
- Red Heart® Boutique™ Sashay® 3.5oz/100g, 30yds/27m (97% acrylic, 3% other fibers)—one each: #1112 Aran (C)
- F-5 (3.75mm) crochet hook
- Black felt and yellow (buttercream) felt [see page 103 for felt templates]
- Fabric glue
- Sewing needle and thread in black

BODY AND HEAD

Rnd 1: With A, 8 sc in adjustable ring—8 sts.

Rnd 2: 2 sc in each st around—16 sts.

Rnds 3–8, 10–13, 17, 19, 21, 23–25: Sc in each st around.

Rnd 9: [Sc in next 3 sts, 2 sc in next st] 4 times—20 sts.

Rnd 14: [Sc in next 3 sts, sc2tog] 4 times—16 sts.

Rnd 15: [Sc in next 2 sts, sc2tog] 4 times—12 sts. Stuff body.

Rnd 16: [Sc in next st, sc2tog] 4 times—8 sts.

Rnd 18: 2 FLsc in each st around—16 sts.

Rnd 20: [Sc in next 3 sts, 2 sc in next st] 4 times—20 sts.

Rnd 22: [Sc in next 4 sts, 2 sc in next st] 4 times—24 sts.

Rnd 26: [Sc in next 4 sts, sc2tog] 4 times—20 sts.

Rnd 27: [Sc in next 3 sts, sc2tog] 4 times—16 sts. Stuff head.

Rnd 28: Sc2tog 8 times—8 sts. Fasten off and close hole.

Cut two eyes from light yellow felt and two pupils from black. Assemble the eyes before gluing or sewing the eyes to the face. With A, apply 3–4 long satin stitches directly across top edge of each eye for eyelids.

HAND AND ARM (make 2)

Rnd 1: With A, 6 sc in adjustable ring—6 sts.

Rnd 2: 2 sc in each st around—12 sts.

Rnds 3–4, 7–10: Sc in each st around.

Rnd 5: [Sc in next st, sc2tog] 4 times—8 sts. Stuff hand.

Rnd 6: [Sc in next 2 sts, sc2tog] 2 times—6 sts.

Rnds 11–12: Hdc in next 2 sts, sl st in next 3 sts, hdc in next st. Stuff lower arm.

Rnds 13–16: Sc in each st around. Stuff upper arm and fasten off. Sew arms to shoulders with elbows pointed back.

LEG AND FOOT (make 2)

Rnd 1: With A, 8 sc in adjustable ring—8 sts.

Rnd 2: 2 sc in each st around—16 sts.

Rnd 3: (Foot Opening) Sc in next 2 sts, sc2tog, sc in next st, ch 6, sk 6 sts, sc in next st, sc2tog, sc in next 2 sts—14 sts.

Rnd 4: Sc2tog, sc in next 2 sts, sc in next 6 ch, sc in next 2 sts, sc2tog—12 sts.

Rnd 5: [Sc in next st, sc2tog] 4 times—8 sts.

Rnds 6–16: Sc in each st around.

Rnd 17: [Sc in next 3 sts, 2 sc in next st] 2 times—10 sts. Fasten off.

FOOT

Rnd 1: Starting in lower right corner of foot opening, join A with (sl st, ch 1, sc) (counts as 1 sc), sc in next 11 sts around inside of foot opening—12 sts.

Rnds 2–3: Sc in each st around.

Rnd 4: [Sc in next 2 sts, 2 sc in next st] 4 times—16 sts.

Rnd 5: Sc in each st around. Fasten off. Stuff foot, flatten and whip st toe edge closed. Stuff leg. With B, embroider smaller toe detail on front of foot.

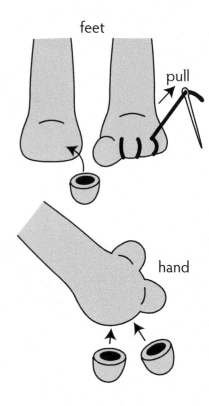

feet

pull

hand

FINGERS AND BIG TOE (make 10)

Rnd 1: With A, 6 sc in adjustable ring—6 sts.

Rnd 2: Sc in each st around. Fasten off. Do not stuff.

Sew open edges of 4 fingers to front edge of each hand and 1 big toe to each foot.

FINISHING

With C, pin the yarn (leaving a 4–5in/10–12.5cm tail) to an arm or leg, wrap the yarn around the limb to cover. Bring the yarn back to the starting point and tie the beginning to the end of the yarn with a square knot. Trim excess, if desired. Repeat on other limbs. When wrapping the head, leave room for the eyes. Wrap the body last.

CTHULHU

Woe to the city by the sea, for Cthulhu is on the move to destroy everything in his path! However, since it's on the way and such a lovely day, he might make a stop at the beach first before he continues on to crush humanity.

SKILL LEVEL
—Advanced Beginner

Height: 8in/20.25cm

- -

MATERIALS

- Berroco Vintage® 3.5oz/100g, 217yds/198m (52% acrylic, 40% wool, 8% nylon)—one each: #5120 Gingham (A), #5112 Minty (B)
- F-5 (3.75mm) crochet hook
- Light green (honeydew) felt, medium green (cabbage) felt and black felt [see page 103 for felt templates]
- Fabric glue
- Sewing needle and thread

BODY

Rnd 1: With A, 8 sc in adjustable ring—8 sts.

Rnd 2: 2 sc in each st around—16 sts.

Rnd 3: [Sc in next 3 sts, 2 sc in next st] 4 times—20 sts.

Rnd 4: [Sc in next st, 2 sc in next st] 10 times—30 sts.

Rnd 5: [Sc in next 2 sts, 2 sc in next st] 10 times—40 sts.

Rnds 6–12, 14, 17–18, 20: Sc in each st around.

Rnd 13: [Sc in next 2 sts, sc2tog] 10 times—30 sts.

Rnd 15: [Sc in next st, sc2tog] 10 times—20 sts.

Rnd 16: [Sc in next 3 sts, 2 sc in next st] 5 times—25 sts.

Rnd 19: [Sc in next 3 sts, sc2tog] 5 times—20 sts.

Rnd 21: [Sc in next 3 sts, sc2tog] 4 times—16 sts.

Rnd 22: Sc in each st around. Stuff body.

Rnd 23: Sc2tog 8 times—8 sts. Fasten off and close hole.

HEAD

Rnd 1: With A, 8 sc in adjustable ring—8 sts.

Rnd 2: 2 Sc in each st around—16 sts.

Rnd 3: [Sc in next 3 sts, 2 sc in next st] 4 times—20 sts.

Rnd 4: [Sc in next st, 2 sc in next st] 10 times—30 sts.

Rnds 5–12, 14: Sc in each st around

Rnd 13: [Sc in next st, sc2tog] 10 times—20 sts.

Rnd 15: Dc in next 5 sts, [sc in next 3 sts, sc2tog] 3 times—17 sts.

Rnd 16: Dc in next 6 sts, sc in next 3 sts, sc2tog, sc in next st, sc2tog, sc in next 3 sts—15 sts.

Rnd 17: Dc in next 6 sts, sc in next 9 sts—15 sts.

Rnd 18: Dc in next 6 sts, sc in next st, [2 sc in next sc, sc in next st] 4 times—19 sts.

Rnd 19: (Tentacles) 1st tentacle—Sc in next st, ch 10, turn, 3 dc in 3rd ch from hook, dc in next 7 ch, sc in same st as last sc at base of ch. 2nd tentacle—Sc in next st, ch 14, turn, 3 dc in 3rd ch from hook, dc in next 11 ch, sc in same st as last sc at base of ch. 3rd & 4th tentacles—[Sc in next st, ch 16, turn, 3 dc in 3rd ch from hook, dc in next 13 ch, sc in same st as last sc at base of ch] 2 times. 5th tentacle—Rep 2nd tentacle. 6th tentacle—Rep 1st tentacle. [Sl st in next st, (sc, 2 hdc, sc) in next st] 6 times, sl st in next st. Fasten off yarn, weave in end.

HEAD TENTACLE UNDERSIDE

Rnd 1: With B, 6 sc in adjustable ring—6 sts.

Rnd 2: 2 sc in each st around—12 sts.

Rnd 3: [Sc in next st, 2 sc in next st] 5 times, 2 sc in next 2 sts—19 sts.

Rnd 4: (Tentacles) Rep Rnd 19 of head. Fasten off.

Stuff head. With WS of tentacle underside facing out match up tentacle edges with head piece and whip stitch tog with A. Stuff before closing seam. Sew head to body.

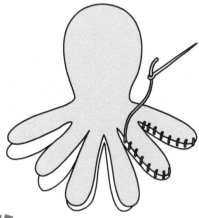

NOSE

Row 1: With B, 8 sc in adjustable ring, turn—8 sts.

Row 2: Ch 1, hdc in each st across. Fasten off.

Sew open edge of nose to head directly above tentacles stuffing lightly before closing seam.

EYE MASK

Rnd 1: With B, ch 8, hdc in 2nd ch from hook, sc in next 3 ch. Ch 13, sc in 2nd ch from hook and next 11 ch, sc in st at base of ch. Sc in next 2 ch of ch-8, 5 hdc in next ch. Rotate ch so front loops are facing up. Sc in next 5 sts, hdc 4 in next st—45 sts.

Rnd 2: 2 sc in next st, sl st in next 30 sts (working in both sides of ch-13), 2 sc in next st, 2 hdc in next 3 sts, 2 sc in next st, sl st in next 5 sts, 2 sc in next st, 2 hdc in next 3 sts—55 sts. Sl st in next st and fasten off.

Sew eye mask to front of face above nose and tack column to the top of the head. Cut two eyes from light green felt, two eyelids from medium green felt, and two pupils from black felt. Assemble eyes before gluing or sewing to eye mask.

BROW

With B, ch 17, hdc in 2nd ch from hook and each st across. Fasten off. Sew eyebrow across top edge of eye mask. Fold center of eyebrow down to the bottom edge of eye mask and secure with a few sts.

ARMS & LEGS (make 4)

Rnd 1: With B, 5 sc in adjustable ring—5 sts.

Rnd 2: 2 sc in each st around—10 sts.

Rnd 3: [2 sc in next st] 3 times, [2 hdc in next st] 4 times, [2 sc in next st] 3 times—20 sts.

Rnd 4: With A, sc in next 6 sts, BLhdc in next st, pm in FL, BLhdc in next 7 sts, sc in next 6 sts.

Rnd 5: Sc in next 6 sts, sc2tog 4 times, sc in next 6 sts—16 st.

Rnds 6–10: Sc in each st around.

Rnd 11: [Sc in next 2 sts, sc2tog] 4 times—12 sts. Stuff limb.

Rnd 12: Sc2tog 6 times—6 sts. Fasten off and close hole. Sew arms and legs to shoulders and hips.

WEBBING

Row 1: Attach A with (sl st, ch 1, sc) in FL of marked st, FLsc in next 7 hdc, turn—8 sts.

Row 2: Ch 1, [(sc, hdc, sc) in next st, sl st] 4 times—16 sts. Fasten off.

*turn and work row 2

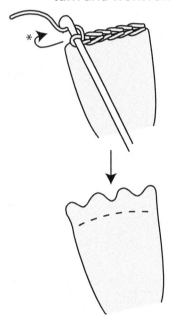

WINGS

Row 1: With A, ch 27, sc in 2nd ch from hook and each ch across—26 sts.

Rows 2–3: Ch 1, sc in each st across, turn.

Row 4: Fold lengthwise holding 1st and 3rd row tog working through both layers, ch 1, sl st in each st across, turn—26 sts.

FIRST WING

Row 5: With B, ch 1, FLsc in next 12 sts, turn—12 sts.

Row 6: Ch 1, hdc in next 6 sts, sc in next 4 sts, turn—10 sts.

Row 7: Ch 1, sc2tog 2 times, hdc in next st, 2 hdc in next st, hdc in next st, sc in next 2 sts, turn—8 sts.

Row 8: Ch 1, sk 1, sc in next 2 sts, hdc in next 2 sts, sc in next st, turn—5 sts.

Row 9: Ch 1, sc2tog, hdc in next 2 sts, sl st, fasten off.

SECOND WING

Row 5: Turn wing and join B with (sl st, ch 1, sc) in opposite end of Row 4, BLsc in each st across, turn—12 sts.

Rows 6–9: Rep as for First Wing. Fasten off.

INNER WINGS

First Wing: Join B in BL at beg of Row 5, rep Rows 5–9.

Second Wing: Join B in FL at beg of Row 5, rep Rows 5–9.

Wing Edging: With inner wing facing, hold inner and outer pieces tog. Join A with (sl st, ch 1, sc) at end of row 5. [Ch 3, sc in sc at base of ch-3 to to make a "wing point." Sc through both edge layers of inner and outer wing to next location where you wish to add a "wing point"] 3 times, sc to end. Fasten off. Rep for Second Wing.

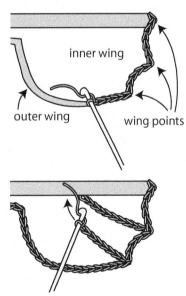

inner wing

outer wing

wing points

RIBBING

With A, sc a line on surface of inner wing from middle wing point of Row 4 for each wing.

Sew center of wings bet shoulders with ribbed side facing forward.

ITSY BITSY

Itsy Bitsy Spider runs up the water spout. Along comes some poor soul who tries to pull her out. Itsy Bitsy Spider suddenly attacks, and the guy who tries to grab her becomes a tasty snack.

SKILL LEVEL
—**Intermediate**

9¾ in/24.75cm
Body Length: 6¼in/16cm

- -

MATERIALS

- Berroco Vintage® 3.5oz/100g, 217yds/198m, (52% acrylic, 40% wool, 8% nylon)—one each: #5182 Black Currant (A), #5188 Juniper (B), #5105 Oats (C), #5145 Cast Iron (D)
- F-5 (3.75mm) crochet hook
- White felt and black felt [see page 103 for felt templates]
- Black pipe cleaners (8)
- Fabric glue
- Sewing needle and thread

BODY

Rnd 1: With B, 8 sc in adjustable ring—8 sts.

Rnd 2: 2 sc in each st around—16 sts.

Rnd 3: [Sc in next st, 2 sc in next st] 8 times—24 sts.

Rnd 4: (leg openings) Sc in next 4 sts, [ch 3, sk 1, sc in next st] 4 times, sc in next 4 sts, [ch 3, sk 1, sc in next st] 4 times—40 sts.

Rnd 5: Ch 6, sk 3 sc, sc in next sc, [sc3tog in ch-3 sts, sc in next st] 4 times, ch 6, sk 3, sc in next st, [sc3tog in ch-3 sts, sc in next st] 4 times—30 sts.

Rnd 6: Sc2tog 3 times in ch-6 sts, sc2tog 4 times, sc in next st, Sc2tog 3 times in ch-6 sts, sc in next st, sc2tog 4 times—16 sts.

8 small openings for legs and 2 large openings for head and abdomen. Pm in large opening closest to hook for abdomen opening. Loosely fasten off. Do not close opening.

FRONT SHORT LEGS

(**Note:** Work in the front 2 small leg openings on either side of the head opening)

Hold body with Rnd 1 facing down. Locate the 2 small openings closest to the head opening.

Rnd 1: Join A in bottom edge of leg opening with (sl st, ch 1, 2 sc) (counts as 2 sc), 2 sc in next 3 sts around opening—8 sts.

Rnd 2: (Sc, FPsc) in next st, FPsc in next 7 sts—9 sts.

Rnd 3: Hold unused color to back of work, do not cut. With B, sk 1, [BLsc in next 2 sts, BLsc-2tog] 2 times—6 sts.

Rnds 4–6: Sc in each st around.

Rnd 7: With A, 2 FPsc in each st around—12 sts.

Rnd 8: With B, BLsc2tog 6 times—6 sts.

Rnds 9–11: Sc in each st around.

Rnds 12-16: Rep Rnds 7–11.

Rnd 17: With A, 2 FPsc in each st around—12 sts.

Rnd 18: [BLsc in next st, BLsc2tog] 4 times—8 sts.

Rnds 19–20: Sc in each st around.

Rnd 21: [Sc in next 2 sts, sc2tog] 2 times—6 sts.

Rnds 22–23: Sc in each st around. Lightly stuff the bottom section of the leg.

Rnd 24: [Sc in next st, sc2tog] 2 times—4 sts. Fasten off. Insert pipe cleaner skeleton (see Tips & Tricks on pages 22–23).

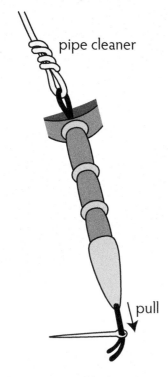

pipe cleaner

pull

BACK LONG LEGS (work in the back 6 small leg openings)

Hold body with Rnd 1 facing down.

Rnds 1–6: Rep Rnds 1–6 of Front Short Legs.

Rnd 7: Sc in each st around.

Rnd 8: With A, 2 FPsc in each st around—12 sts.

Rnd 9: With B, BLsc2tog 6 times—6 sts.

Rnds 10–13: Sc in each st around.

Rnds 14–19: Rep Rnds 8–13.

Rnd 20: With A, 2 FPsc in each st around—12 sts.

Rnd 21: [BLsc in next st, BLsc2tog] 4 times—8 sts.

Rnds 22–24: Sc in each st around.

Rnd 25: [Sc in next 2 sts, sc2tog] 2 times—6 sts.

Rnds 26–27: Sc in each st around. Lightly stuff the bottom section of leg.

Rnd 28: [Sc in next st, sc2tog] 2 times—4 sts. Fasten off. Insert pipe cleaner skeleton (see Tips & Tricks on pages 22–23).

CLOSE BODY

Rnd 7: With B, sc in each st around—16 sts.

Rnd 8: [Sc in next 2 sts, sc2tog] 4 times—12 sts. Stuff body.

Rnd 9: [Sc in next st, sc2tog] 4 times—8 sts. Fasten off and close hole at top of body.

ABDOMEN

Remove marker from large opening in body to work in this opening. Hold body with Rnd 1 facing down.

Rnd 1: Join B in bottom corner of abdomen opening with (sl st, ch 1, 2 sc) (counts as 2 sc), 2 sc in each st around inside of abdomen opening—18 sts.

Rnds 2, 4, 6–8, 10–11, 13, 15: Sc in each st around.

Rnd 3: [Sc in next st, 2 sc in next st] 8 times—27 sts.

Rnd 5: [Sc in next 2 sts, 2 sc in next st] 8 times—36 sts.

Rnd 9: [Sc in next 4 sts, sc2tog] 6 times—30 sts.

Rnd 12: [Sc in next 3 sts, sc2tog] 6 times—24 sts.

Rnd 14: [Sc in next 2 sts, sc2tog] 6 times—18 sts.

Rnd 16: [Sc in next st, sc2tog] 6 times—12 sts. Stuff abdomen.

Rnd 17: Sc2tog 6 times—6 sts. Fasten off and close hole.

FANGS (make 2)

Rnd 1: With C, 6 sc in adjustable ring—6 sts.

Rnds 2–3: Sc in each st around.

Rnds 4–5: Sl st in next 2 sts, hdc in next 3 sts, sl st in next st.

Rnd 6: Sc in each st around. Fasten off. Stuff fangs.

With fangs curving down, insert Rnd 5 of fangs in opening in front of body, sew in place with B.

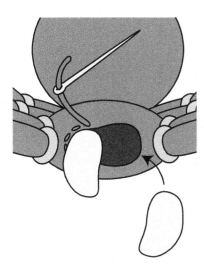

Rnds 2–3: Sc in each st around. Fasten off.

Place eye bases in a row across the middle of WS of eyecase with 2 larger eye bases in the center and the smaller eye bases on either side. Sew bases to the inside surface of the eye case. Allow the edge of the eye case to wrap around the eyes like peas in a pod. Tack the edge of eye case to the sides of the eyes.

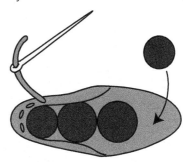

EYE BASE SMALL (make 2)

Rnd 1: With D, 4 sc in adjustable ring—4 sts.

Rnd 2: [Sc in next st, 2 sc in next st] 2 times—6 sts.

Rnd 3: [Sc in next st, sc2tog] 2 times—4 sts. Fasten off.

EYE BASE LARGE (make 2)

Rnd 1: With D, 6 sc in adjustable ring—6 sts.

Rnd 2: [Sc in next 2 sts, 2 sc in next st] 2 times—8 sts.

Rnd 3: Sc in each st around.

Rnd 4: [Sc in next 2 sts, sc2tog] 2 times—6 sts. Stuff and fasten off.

EYE CASE

Rnd 1: With B, ch 10, sc in 2nd ch from hook and next 7 ch, 4 sc next ch. Rotate ch so front loops are facing up. Sc in next 7 ch, 3 sc in next ch—22 sts.

Attach completed eye case to top of body behind the fangs.

Cut two large eyes and two small eyes from black felt and two large sets of pupils and two small sets of pupils from white felt. Assemble eyes and glue or sew to eye bases.

Cut eight 4in/10cm pieces of B and attach fringe bet eyes and fangs. Use a tapestry needle to separate yarn plies and trim to desired length.

SPINNERETS (make 2)

Rnd 1: With C, 3 sc in adjustable ring—3 sts

Rnd 2: 2 sc in each st around—6 sts.

Rnds 3–4: Sl st in next 2 sts, hdc in next 3 sts, sl st in next st. Fasten off and stuff.

Sew open edges to end of abdomen with points curved in.

WEREWOLF DAVE

Poor Dave. He's always forgetting NOT to wear his nice clothes on the nights when the full moon is up. There goes another shirt!

SKILL LEVEL
—**Intermediate**

Height: 7½in/19cm, including ears

- - - - - - - - - - - - - - - - - - - -

MATERIALS

- Lion Brand® Wool Ease® 3oz/85g,197yds/180m (80% acrylic, 20% wool)—one each: #129 Cocoa (A), #403 Mushroom (B), #098 Natural Heather (C), #114 Denim (D), #153 Black (E)
- Lion Brand® Pelt 1.75oz/50g, 47yds/43m (68% Nylon, 32% Polyester) in #205 Sable (F)
- F-5 (3.75mm) crochet hook
- Black felt and light yellow (buttercream) felt [see page 103 for felt templates]
- Fabric glue
- Sewing needle and thread

HEAD

Rnd 1: With A, ch 9, sc in 2nd ch from hook and in next 6 ch, 5 sc in next ch. Rotate ch so front loops are facing up. Sc in next 6 ch, 4 sc in next ch—22 sts.

Rnd 2: 2 hdc in next st, sc in next 6 sts, 2 hdc in next 5 sts, sc in next 6 sts, 2 hdc in next 4 sts—32 sts.

Rnd 3: Sc in next 11 sts, 2 hdc in next 4 sts, sc in next 12 sts, 2 hdc in next 4 sts, sc in next st—40 sts.

Rnds 4–7, 9–10, 12: Sc in each st around.

Rnd 8: [Sc in next 2 sts, sc2tog] 10 times—30 sts.

Rnd 11: [Sc in next st, sc2tog] 10 times—20 sts.

Rnd 13: Sc2tog 10 times—10 sts. Fasten off and stuff head.

MUZZLE

Rnd 1: With B, ch 8, sc in 2nd ch from hook and in next 5 ch, 3 sc in next ch. Rotate ch so front loops are facing up. Sc in next 5 sts, 2 sc in next st—16 sts.

Rnd 2: [Sc in next 3 sts, 2 sc in next st] 4 times—20 sts.

Rnds 3–4: Sc in each st around.

Rnd 5: [Sc in next 3 sts, sc2tog] 4 times—16 sts.

Rnd 6: Sc in each st around. Fasten off and stuff muzzle.

Sew open edge of muzzle to center of head. Stuff lightly and close seam. With B, add lip cleft to muzzle as illustrated.

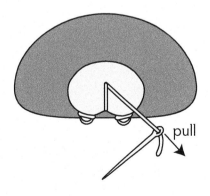

pull

FANGS

With C, work a chunky French knot on each side of the muzzle. Wrap yarn around base of the French knot 4–5 times and thread needle through knot to secure.

FACE

Rnd 1: With B, ch 8, sc in 2nd ch from hook and in next 5 ch, 5 sc in next ch. Rotate ch so front loops are facing up. Sc in next 5 sts, 4 sc in next st—20 sts.

Rnd 2: 2 hdc in next st, sc in next 5 sts, 2 hdc in next 2 sts, (sl st, ch 3, sl st at base of ch) in next 3 sts, sl st in next 5 sts, (sl st, ch 3, sl st at base of ch) in next 3 sts, 2 hdc in next st—30 sts. Fasten off. Sew face to head with sl st edge flush against top edge of muzzle.

Cut two eyes from light yellow felt and two sets of pupils from black felt. Assemble eyes and glue or sew to face.

EYEBROW

Row 1: With A, ch 11, 2 sc in 2nd ch from hook, sc in next 8 ch, 2 sc in next ch, turn—12 sts.

Row 2: Ch 1, 2 sc in next 2 sts, hdc in next 2 sts, sc in next st, sl st in next 2 sts, sc in next st, hdc in next 2 sts, 2 sc in next 2 sts, turn—16 sts.

Row 3: Ch 1, sc in next 4 sts, hdc in next 2 sts, sc in next st, sl st in next 2 sts, sc in next st, hdc in next 2 sts, sc in next 4 sts, turn.

Row 4: Ch 1, sc2tog 2 times, hdc in next 2 sts, sc in next st, sl st in next 2 sts, sc in next st, hdc in next 2 sts, sc2tog 2 times—12 sts.

Row 5: Fold eyebrow the long way matching up Rows 1 and 4. Sl st through both layers in each st across. Fasten off. Sew sl st edge of eyebrows along top of eyes, covering top portion of face above eyes.

JAW

Rnd 1: With B, ch 5, sc in 2nd ch from hook and in next 2 ch, 3 sc in next ch. Rotate ch so front loops are facing up. Sc in next 2 sts, 2 sc in next st—10 sts.

Rnds 2–3: Sc in each st across.

Rnd 4: [Sc in next st, 2 sc in next st] 5 times—15 sts. Stuff lightly. Fasten off. Sew open edge of jaw directly below muzzle, stuff firmly and close seam. Tack sides of muzzle to sides of jaw.

NOSE

Row 1: With E, ch 4, 5 sc in 2nd ch from hook, sc in next ch, sc 5 in next ch, turn—11 sts.

Row 2: Ch 1, sl st in each st across. Fasten off. Sew nose to front of muzzle. Work 4-6 satin sts over the front of the nose (through the cleft) and back up again. Work 3 satin sts over the sides of the nose by the nostrils pulling gently to shape the openings. With E, draw a long st over lip cleft to highlight it.

EARS (make 2)

Rnd 1: With A, ch 5, sc in 2nd ch from hook and in next 2 ch, 5 hdc in next ch. Rotate ch so front loops are facing up. FLsc in next 2 sts, 2 FLsc in next ch—12 sts.

Rnd 2: Ch 3, sl st in next 2 sts, sc in next st, hdc in next 5 sts, sc in next st, sl st in next 3 sts.

Sl st in ch-3 sp to join. Fasten off. Sew rounded ends of ears to top of head. Work a small stitch of F inside base of ears and 3-4 clustered sts to top of head. Loosen and fluff fur.

SHORTS AND BELLY

Rnd 1: With D, ch 9, sc in 2nd ch from hook and next 6 sc, 5 sc in next ch. Rotate ch so front loops are facing up. Sc in next 6 sts, 4 sc in next ch—22 sts.

Rnd 2: 2 sc in next st, sc in next 6 sts, 2 sc in next 5 sts, sc in next 6 sts, 2 sc in next 4 sts—32 sts.

Rnd 3: Sc in next 11 sts, 2 sc in next 4 sts, sc in next 12 sts, 2 sc in next 4 sts, sc in next st—40 sts.

Rnds 4–5: Sc in each st around.

Rnd 6: With A, BLsc in each st around.

Rnds 7–9: Sc in each st around. Fasten off.

SHIRT

With C, ch 40, join with a sl st to form a ring.

Rnd 1: Ch 1, 40 sc in ring—40 sts.

Rnd 2: Slip ring over open edge of shorts and belly. Line up Rnd 9 of belly with Rnd 1 of shirt. Working through both layers, sc in each st around—40 sts.

Rnds 3, 5: Sc in each st around.

Rnd 4: [Sc in next 2 sts, sc2tog] 10 times—30 sts.

Rnd 6: [Sc in next st, sc2tog] 10 times—20 sts.

Rnd 7: With A, BLsc in each st around.

Rnd 8: Sc2tog 10 times—10 sts. Fasten off and stuff body. Sew head to body.

LEG (make 2)

Rnd 1: With A, 8 sc in adjustable ring—8 sts.

Rnd 2: 2 sc in each st around—16 sts.

Rnd 3: (foot opening) 2 BLsc in next st, BLsc in next 3 sts, 2 BLsc in next st, ch 6, sk 6 sts, 2 BLsc in next st, BLsc in next 3 sts, 2 BLsc in next st—20 sts.

Rnd 4: Sc in next 7 sts, sc in next 6 ch, sc in next 7 sts—20 sts.

Rnd 5: [Sc in next 3 sts, sc2tog] 4 times—16 sts.

Rnd 6: Sc in each st around.

Rnd 7: [Sc in next 2 sts, sc2tog] 4 times—12 sts.

Rnd 8: Sc in each st around. Fasten off.

FOOT (make 2)

Rnd 1: Join A to leg in lower right corner of foot opening with (sl st, ch 1, sc) (counts as 1 sc), sc in next 11 sts around inside of foot opening—12 sts.

Rnd 2: [Sc in next st, 2 sc in next st] 6 times—18 sts.

Rnd 3: [Sc in next 2 sts, 2 sc in next st] 6 times—24 sts.

Rnd 4: Sc in each st around.

Rnd 5: [Sc in next 2 sts, sc2tog] 6 times—18 sts. Fasten off. Flatten and whip stitch toe edge closed.

SHORT PANT LEG (make 2)

With D, ch 14, join with a sl st to form a ring.

Rnd 1: Ch 1, [sc in next 5 sts, sc2tog] 2 times—12 sts.

Rnd 2: Slip short pant leg ring over the open edge of leg. Line up Rnd 8 of leg with Rnd 1 of shorts. Working through both layers, sc in each st around—12 sts.

Rnd 3: [Sc in next 3 sts, 2 sc in next st] 3 times—15 sts. Fasten off.

Stuff leg and sew open edge to bottom of body.

HAND AND ARM (make 2)

Rnd 1: With A, 8 sc in adjustable ring—8 sts.

Rnd 2: 2 sc in each st around—16 sts.

Rnd 3: [Sc in next 3 sts, 2 sc in next st] 4 times—20 sts.

Rnds 4, 6: Sc in each st around.

Rnd 5: [Sc in next 3 sts, sc2tog] 4 times—16 sts.

Rnd 7: [Sc in next 2 sts, sc2tog] 4 times—12 sts.

Rnds 8–9: Sc in each st around. Stuff arm and fasten off.

SLEEVE (make 2)

With C, ch 14, join with a sl st to form a ring.

Rnd 1: Ch 1, [sc in next 5 sts, sc2tog] 2 times—12 sts.

Rnd 2: Slip sleeve ring over open edge of arm. Line up Rnd 9 of arm with Rnd 1 of sleeve. Working through both layers, sc in each st around—12 sts.

Rnd 3: [Sc in next 3 sts, 2 sc in next st] 3 times—15 sts.

Rnd 4: Sc2tog 2 times, hdc in next 7 sts, sc2tog 2 times—11 sts.

Rnd 5: Sl st in next 2 sts, hdc in next 7 sts, sl st in next 2 sts—11 sts. Fasten off.

Stuff arm, flatten seam and sew closed. Sew to shoulders.

THUMB (make 2)

Rnd 1: With A, 6 sc in adjustable ring—6 sts.

Rnd 2: Sc in each st around. Fasten off. Do not stuff.

Sew open edges of thumb to hand.

TAIL

Rnd 1: With A, 4 sc in adjustable ring—4 sts.

Rnd 2: [Sc in next st, 2 sc in next st] 2 times—6 sts.

Rnd 3: [Sc in next 2 sts, 2 sc in next st] 2 times—8 sts.

Rnd 4: [Sc in next st, 2 sc in next st] 4 times—12 sts.

Rnd 5: [Sc in next 2 sts, 2 sc in next st] 4 times—16 sts.

Rnds 6, 8–10: Sc in each st around.

Rnd 7: [Sc in next 2 sts, sc2tog] 4 times—12 sts.

Rnd 11: [Sc in next st, sc2tog] 4 times—8 sts.

Rnds 12–13: Sc in each st around.

Stuff just the end of the tail firmly (use the handle of the crochet hook to push in stuffing, if needed).

Rnd 14: [Sc in next 2 sts, sc2tog] 2 times—6 sts. Fasten off.

Sew tail to back of pants. With F, backstitch around the base of the tail.

FINISHING

With E, work 3 long sts on front edges of feet and hands and cinch to form toes and fingers.

With C make 1–2 small satin sts at front of each toe, finger, and thumb for claws.

With matching yarn, tack cuffs and hem of shirt in place, if desired.

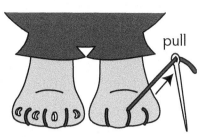

With F, backstitch around edge of muzzle and face 2 times. Draw one long strand of F across face bet eyebrows and eyes. Backstitch around base of neck 2 times. Backstitch 1 to 2 lines around circumference of leg and arm under cuffs of sleeve and pant leg. Use fingers or a comb to loosen fur.

SWAMP THANG

Swamp Thang is looking sexy, sassy (and a bit slimy) in her pink bikini. It's a shame that everyone always runs away when she shows up to strut her stuff on the beach, but at least she'll have the surf, sand, and sun all to herself.

SKILL LEVEL
—Intermediate

Height: 6½in/16.5cm, including ears

- - - - - - - - - - - - - - - - - - - -

MATERIALS

- Berroco® Vintage® 3½oz/100g, 217yds/198m (52% acrylic, 40% wool, 8% nylon)—one each: #5102 Buttercream (A), #5145 Cast Iron (B), #5126 Watermelon (C), #5114 Aster (D), #5124 Kiwi (E), #51103 Clary (F)
- F-5 (3.75mm) crochet hook
- Black felt and light yellow (buttercream) felt [see page 103 for felt templates]
- Fabric glue
- Sewing needle and thread in black and light yellow

HEAD

Rnd 1: With E, ch 7, sc in 2nd ch from hook and in next 4 ch, 5 sc in next ch. Rotate ch so front loops are facing up. Sc in next 4 sts, 4 sc in next ch—18 sts.

Rnd 2: 2 hdc in next st, sc in next 4 sts, 2 hdc in next 5 sts, sc in next 4 sts, 2 hdc in next 4 sts—28 sts.

Rnd 3: 2 hdc in next 2 sts, sc in next 4 sts, 2 hdc in next 10 sts, sc in next 4 sts, 2 hdc in next 8 sts—48 sts.

Rnds 4–5, 10–11: Sc in each st around.

Rnd 6: [Sc in next 4 sts, sc2tog] 8 times—40 sts.

Rnd 7: [Sc in next 8 sts, sc2tog] 4 times—36 sts.

Rnd 8: [Sc in next 4 sts, sc2tog] 6 times—30 sts.

Rnd 9: [Sc in next st, sc2tog] 10 times—20 sts.

Rnd 12: [Sc in next 3 sts, sc2tog] 4 times—16 sts. Stuff head.

Rnd 13: Sc2tog 8 times—8 sts. Fasten off and finish stuffing head.

MOUTH

With A, ch 20, join with a slip stitch to form a ring.

Rnd 1: Ch 1, 20 sc in ring—20 sts.

Rnds 2–4: Sc in each st around. Fasten off.

Whip st Rnd 1 to Rnd 4 to create a tube. Flatten and sew edges together. Place stitched edge against head and sew mouth to face in a frown shape. With B, work 1–2 long sts over the space bet top and bottom lip.

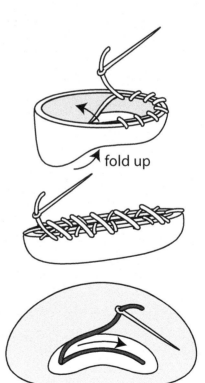

fold up

EYE BASES (make 2)

Rnd 1: With F, 6 sc in adjustable ring—6 sts.

Rnd 2: [Sc in next 2 sts, 2 sc in next st] 2 times—8 sts.

Rnd 3: Sc in each st around. Fasten off.

Stuff eye bases and sew to front of head above mouth. Cut two eyes from light yellow felt and two pupils from black felt. Assemble eyes and glue or sew eyes to eye bases. With B, embroider 2 sts above each eye for eyebrows.

EARS (make 2)

Row 1: With D, 7 sc in adjustable ring, turn—7 sts.

Row 2: Ch 1, sk 1, sl st in next st, (sc, hdc, ch 2, sl st in in 2nd ch from hook, sc) in next 3 sts, sl st in next 2 sts, turn.

Row 3: With E, ch 1, sl st in each st across. Fasten off.

Sew ears to sides of head. With E, work 3 long sts radiating from the base of ear to the 3 points along the edge of Row 3.

HEAD FIN

Row 1: With D, ch 10. Starting in 2nd ch from hook, [sl st in next st, (Sc, hdc, ch 2, sl st in in 2nd ch from hook, sc) in next st, sl st in next st] 3 times, turn.

Row 2: With E, sc in each st across. Fasten off.

Sew row 1 edge to top and back of head. With E, work 3 long sts radiating from the base of the head fin to the 3 highest points.

BODY

Rnd 1: With E, 8 sc in adjustable ring—8 sts.

Rnd 2: 2 sc in each st around—16 sts.

Rnd 3: [Sc in next st, 2 sc in next st] 8 times—24 sts.

Rnd 4: [Sc in next 2 sts, 2 sc in next st] 8 times—32 sts.

Rnd 5: [Sc in next 3 sts, 2 sc in next st] 8 times—40 sts.

Rnd 6: [Sc in next 4 sts, 2 sc in next st] 8 times—48 sts.

Rnds 7–8, 10, 12, 14: Sc in each st around.

Rnd 9: [Sc in next 4 sts, sc2tog] 8 times—40 sts.

Rnd 11: [Sc in next 3 sts, sc2tog] 8 times—32 sts.

Rnd 13: [Sc in next 2 sts, sc2tog] 8 times—24 sts.

Rnd 15: [Sc in next st, sc2tog] 8 times—16 sts. Stuff body.

Rnd 16: Sc2tog 8 times—8 sts. Fasten off and close hole. Sew head to top of body.

BELLY

Rnd 1: With A, 6 sc in adjustable ring—6 sts.

Rnd 2: 2 sc in each st around—12 sts.

Rnd 3: [Sc in next st, 2 sc in next st] 6 times—18 sts.

Rnd 4: [Sc in next 2 sts, 2 sc in next st] 6 times—24 sts.

Rnd 5: Sc in each st around. Fasten off. Sew belly to front of body. With F, work 4 horizontal long sts across front of belly and pull gently to create shaping.

ARM (make 2)

Rnd 1: With E, 6 sc in adjustable ring—6 sts.

Rnd 2: [Sc in next st, 2 sc in next st] 3 times—9 sts.

Rnds 3, 5–6: Sc in each st around.

Rnd 4: [Sc in next st, sc2tog] 3 times—6 sts.

Rnd 7: [Sc in next st, 2 sc in next st] 3 times—9 sts.

Rnd 8: [Sl st in next st, ch 5, sl st in 2nd ch from hook and next 3 ch] 3 times to make 3 fingers. Sl st in next st, change to D, (sl st, ch 3, hdc, sc, hdc, ch 3, sl st) in next st, change to E, sl st in next 2 sts, change to D (sl st, ch 3, hdc, sc, hdc, ch 3, sl st) in next st, change to E, sl st in next st. Fasten off and stuff arm.

Flatten and press fingers and webbing of hand together. With E, sew sides of webbing to sides of middle finger first, then sew the remaining sides of the webbing to the inside edges of the remaining fingers.

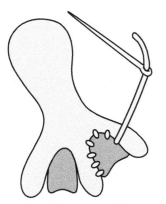

LEG AND FOOT (make 2)
LEG

Rnd 1: With E, 8 sc in adjustable ring—8 sts.

Rnd 2: 2 sc in each st around—16 sts.

Rnd 3: (foot opening) Sc in next 2 sts, sc2tog, sc in next st, ch 6, sk 6, sc in next st, sc2tog, sc in next 2 sts—14 sts.

Rnd 4: Sc2tog, sc in next 2 sts, sc in next 6 ch, sc in next 2 sts, sc2tog—12 sts.

Rnd 5: [Sc in next st, sc2tog] 4 times—8 sts.

Rnds 6–8: Sc in each st around.

Rnd 9: [Sc in next st, 2 sc in next st] 4 times—12 sts.

Rnd 10: [Sc in next 2 sts, 2 sc in next st] 4 times—16 sts.

Rnd 11: [Sc in next 2 sts, sc2tog] 4 times—12 sts. Stuff leg.

Rnd 12: [Sc in next st, sc2tog] 4 times—8 sts.

Rnd 13: [Sc in next 2 sts, sc2tog] 2 times—6 sts. Fasten off.

FOOT

Rnd 1: Starting in lower corner of foot opening, join E with (sl st, ch 1, sc) (counts as 1 sc), sc in next 11 sts around inside of foot opening—12 sts.

Rnds 2–3: Sc in each st around.

Rnd 4: [Sc in next 2 sts, 2 sc in next st] 4 times—16 sts.

Rnd 5: Sc in each st around. Fasten off. Stuff foot lightly.

TOE DETAIL

Row 1: Starting in the lower right corner, and with E, (sl st, ch 1, sc) through sts of top and bottom foot layer at the same time (counts as 1 sc). Working through both layers, sc in next 7 sts across front of foot, turn—8 sts.

Row 2: Ch 1, [(sc, hdc, ch 2, sl st in 2nd ch from hook, hdc, sc) in next st, sl st in next 2 sts] 2 times, (sc, hdc, ch 2, sl st in 2nd ch from hook, hdc, sc) in next st, sl st in next st. Fasten off. Stuff leg. Flatten rounded hip and sew edge to side of body.

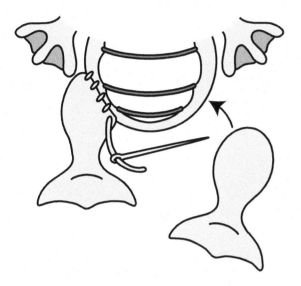

TAIL

Rnd 1: With E, 4 sc in adjustable ring—4 sts.

Rnd 2: [Sc in next st, 2 sc in next st] 2 times—6 sts.

Rnds 3, 5–6, 8–9: Sc in each st around.

Rnd 4: [Sc in next 2 sts, 2 sc in next st] 2 times—8 sts.

Rnd 7: [Sc in next 3 sts, 2 sc in next st] 2 times—10 sts.

Rnd 10: [Sc in next 4 sts, 2 sc in next st] 2 times—12 sts. Fasten off. Stuff tail and sew open edge to back of body.

TAIL FINS (make 2)

Row 1: With D, 7 sc in adjustable ring, turn—7 sts.

Row 2: Ch 1, sk 1, sl st in next st, (sc, ch 2, sl st in 2nd ch from hook, sc) in next 3 sts, sl st in next 2 st, turn.

Row 3: With E, ch 1, sl st in each st across. Fasten off. Sew fins to sides of tail near the tip. With E, work 3 long sts radiating from the base of the tail fin to the 3 points along the edge of row 2.

BIKINI TOP (make 2)

Row 1: With C, 7 sc in adjustable ring, turn—7 sts.

Row 2: Ch 1, sc in next 3 sts, 3 hdc in next st, sc in next 3 sts—9 sts.

Work 4 sl sts across bottom edge. Fasten off.

BIKINI STRAPS

Join yarn at corner of triangle, ch 2 and attach to matching corner of 2nd triangle, fasten off. Join yarn at each of the other 4 corners and ch 15–18 sts for straps. Sew bikini triangles to front of body, tie straps at back of neck and back of body. Weave in ends.

BIKINI BOTTOM

Rnd 1: With C, 8 sc in adjustable ring—8 sts.

Rnd 2: 2 sc in each st around—16 sts.

Rnd 3: [Sc in next st, 2 sc in next st] 8 times—24 sts.

Rnd 4: [Sc in next 2 sts, 2 sc in next st] 8 times—32 sts.

Rnd 5: Sc in next 3 sts, ch 4, sk 4, sc in next 14 sts, ch 4, sk 4, sc in next 3 sts, ch 4, sk 4—32 sts.

Rnd 6: Sc in next 3 sts, sc in next 4 ch, sc in next 14 sts, sc in next 4 ch, sc in next 3 sts, sc in next 4 ch. Fasten off. Slide legs and tail into the 3 openings in Rnd 5. Sew bikini bottom in place.

COUNT VLAD

Count Vlad figured he would go unnoticed when he went out to attend a midnight matinee at his local movie theater. However, management thought he was an usher trying to slack off at work and put poor Vlad at the Box Office to collect ticket stubs instead!

SKILL LEVEL
—Intermediate

Height: 10in/25.5cm

- - - - - - - - - - - - - - - - -

MATERIALS

- Cascade 220® 3.5oz/100g, 220yds/200m (100% Peruvian Highland Wool)—one each: #8555 Black (A), #8505 White (B), #8010 Natural (C), #9404 Ruby (D), #2415 Sunflower (E)
- F-5 (3.75mm) crochet hook
- Dark red (beet) felt, light yellow (sunshine) felt, white felt, and black felt [see page 103 for felt templates]
- Fabric glue
- Sewing needle and thread

HEAD

Rnd 1: With C, 8 sc in adjustable ring—8 sts.

Rnd 2: 2 sc in each st around—16 sts.

Rnd 3: BLsc in each st around.

Rnds 4, 6, 8, 12, 14–15: Sc in each st around.

Rnd 5: [Sc in next 3 sts, 2 sc in next st] 4 times—20 sts.

Rnd 7: [Sc in next 4 sts, 2 sc in next st] 4 times—24 sts.

Rnd 9: Sc in next 6 sts, 2 hdc in next 2 sts, sc in next 8 sts, 2 hdc in next 2 sts, sc in next st 6 sts—28 sts.

Rnd 10: Sc in next 6 sts, sc2tog 2 times, sc in next 4 sts, pm, sc in next 4 sts, sc2tog 2 times, sc in next 6 sts—24 sts.

Rnd 11: [Sc in next 4 sts, sc2tog] 4 times—20 sts.

Rnd 13: [Sc in next 3 sts, sc2tog] 4 times—16 sts.

Rnd 16: [Sc in next 2 sts, sc2tog] 4 times—12 sts.

Rnds 17–18: Sc 12. Fasten off. Marker indicates center of face. Stuff head. Flatten chin seam and sew closed with a mattress stitch.

NOSE

Rnd 1: With C, 4 sc in adjustable ring—4 sts.

Rnd 2: Sc in next st, 2 hdc in next 2 sts, sc in next st—6 sts.

Row 3: 2 sc in next st, sc2tog 2 times, 2 sc in next st, turn—6 sts.

Row 4: Ch 1, sc in each st across, turn—6 sts.

Row 5: Ch 1, sc in next 2 sts, sc2tog, sc in next 2 sts—5 sts. Fasten off.

Stuff tip of nose. Sew edges to center of face (remove marker). Pinch face above nose to form a nose bridge. Work running sts through nose bridge to secure.

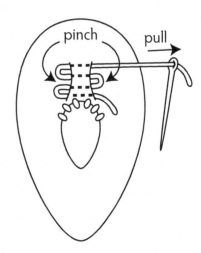

Cut two eyes from light yellow felt and two pupils from dark red felt. Assemble the eyes and glue or sew to the face. With C, work 3–4 long satin sts directly across the top edge of each eye for eyelids.

With A, embroider upper lip outline (pulling firmly to shape upper lip), mouth, and eyelash detail. Double yarn to embroider eyebrows. Cut 2 fangs from white felt and 2 fangs from black felt. Glue the white fangs to the black fangs, then glue or sew the fangs under the mouth.

pull gently

HAIR

Rnd 1: With A, 8 sc in adjustable ring—8 sts.

Rnd 2: 2 sc in next 7 sts, sc in next st—15 sts.

Rnd 3: BLsc in next 5 sts, BLsl st in next 2 sts, (sc, hdc, ch 2, sl st in back ridge loop in 2nd ch from hook, hdc, sc) in BL of next st (counts as 1 st), BLsl st in next 2 sts, BLsc in next 5 sts. PM in 5th st from hook—15 sts. Fasten off.

Rnd 4: Rejoin A (Sl st, ch 1, sc) in marked st (counts as 1 st), sc in next 9 sts, turn—10 sts.

Row 5: Ch 1, sc in next 10 sts, turn.

Row 6: Ch 1, 2 hdc in next st, sl st in next st, sc in next 6 sts, sl st in next st, 2 hdc in next st, turn.

Row 7: Ch 1, sl st in next 3 sts, sc in next 6 sts, turn—9 sts.

Rows 8–10: Ch 1, sc in next 6 sts, turn—6 sts.

Row 11: Ch 1, sc in next 2 sts, (hdc, dc) in next st, (dc, hdc) in next st, sc in next 2 sts—8 sts. Fasten off. With marker in center of forehead, sew edge of hair to top of head.

LEFT EAR

Row 1: With C, 4 sc in adjustable ring. Do not join, turn—4 sts.

Row 2: Ch 1, sl st in next 3 sts, (sc, hdc, ch 2, sl st in 2nd ch from hook, sc) in next st. Fasten off.

RIGHT EAR

Row 1: With C, 4 sc in adjustable ring. Do not join, turn—4 sts.

Row 2: Ch 1, (sc, hdc, ch 2, sl st in back ridge loop in 2nd ch from hook, sc) in next st, sl st 3. Fasten off.

Sew ears to sides of head with point at the top.

BODY

Rnd 1: With B, ch 8, sc in 2nd ch from hook and in next 5 ch, 5 sc in next ch. Rotate ch so front loops are facing up. Sc in next 5 sts, 4 sc in next ch—20 sts.

Rnd 2: 2 hdc in next st, sc in next 5 sts, 2 hdc in next 5 sts, sc in next 5 sts, 2 hdc in next 4 sts—30 sts.

Rnds 3–5, 7–9, 11–13, 15–17, 19: Sc in each st around.

Rnd 6: [Sc in next 4 sts, sc2tog] 5 times—25 sts.

Rnd 10: [Sc in next 3 sts, sc2tog] 5 times—20 sts.

Rnd 14: [Sc in next 2 sts, sc2tog] 5 times—15 sts.

Rnd 18: With A, FPsc in each st around.

Rnd 20: [Sc in next 4 sts, 2 sc in next st] 3 times—18 sts.

Rnd 21: Sc2tog 9 times—9 sts. Fasten off. Stuff body. Flatten seam and sew shut. Sew head to upper front half of body.

VEST BACK

Row 1: With A, ch 9, sc in 2nd ch from hook and each ch across, turn—8 sts.

Rows 2–5, 7–9, 11–16: Ch 1, sc in each st across, turn.

Row 6: Ch 1, [2 sc in next st, sc in next st] 2 times, [sc in next st, 2 sc in next st] 2 times, turn—12 sts.

Row 10: Ch 1, sc2tog, sc in next 8 sts, sc2tog, turn—10 sts.

Row 17: Ch 1, 3 sc in next st, sc in next 8 sts, 3 sc in next st, turn—14 sts. Fasten off.

VEST FRONT

Row 1: With D, ch 13, sc in 2nd ch from hook and each ch across, turn—12 sts.

Rows 2–5, 8–18: Ch 1, sc in each st across, turn.

Row 6: Ch 1, sc in next 4 sts, sl st in next 4 sts, sc in next 4 sts. Pm in beg of row, turn—12 sts.

Row 7: Ch 1, sc in next 2 sts, sc2tog, turn, leaving rem sts unworked—3 sts.

Row 19: Ch 1, 2 sc in next st, sc in next 2 sts, turn—4 sts.

Row 20: Ch 1, hdc in next 2 sts, sc in next 2 sts, turn.

Row 21: Ch 1, sc in next 2 sts, hdc in next 2 sts. Fasten off.

Join yarn in marked stitch and rep Rows 7–21. Fasten off.

Work sc on surface of vest for an overlap detail. Cut 4 buttons from white felt and attach to front of vest. Sew shoulders and side seams to Row 9 of back. Insert body and tack vest to body with D.

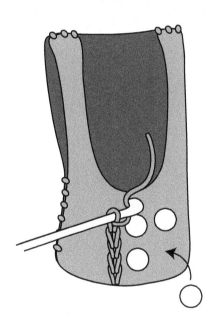

AMULET

Rnd 1: With D, 6 sc in adjustable ring—6 sts.

Rnd 2: With E, [sl st in next st, ch 3, sl st in st at base of ch] 6 times. Fasten off.

NECKLACE

With D, ch 25, sl st in 2nd ch from hook and next 3 ch, sc in next 4 ch, hdc in next 8 ch, sc in next 4 ch, sl st in next 4 ch. Fasten off. Drape necklace around neck overlapping end points in the middle of the chest. Sew in place. Sew amulet over overlap point and weave in ends.

CAPE

Row 1: With A, ch 20, sc in 2nd ch from hook and next 18 ch, turn—19 sts.

Rows 2–5: Ch 1, sc2tog, sc across to last 2 sts, sc2tog, turn—11 sts.

Row 6, Ch 1, sc 11, ch 4, turn—11 sts.

Row 7: Starting in 2nd ch from hook, sc 3 in ch, sc 11, ch 4 and turn—14 sts.

Row 8: Starting in 2nd ch from hook, sc 3 in next 3 ch, sc 14, turn—17 sts.

Rows 9–10: Ch 1, 2 sc in next st, sc across to last st, 2 sc in last st, turn—21sts.

Rows 11–34: Ch 1, sc in each st across, turn.

Row 35: Ch 1, [(sc, hdc, ch 2, sl st in 2nd ch from hook, hdc, sc) in next st (counts as 1 st), sl st in next 3 sts] 5 times, (sc, hdc, ch 2, sl st in in 2nd ch from hook, hdc, sc) in next st (counts as 1 st)—21 sts. Fasten off. Block cape with a low heat iron, if desired. Sew Row 6 to shoulders behind head.

SHOE AND LEG (make 2)

Rnd 1: With A, 4 sc in adjustable ring, turn—4 sts.

Rnd 2: [Sc in next st, 2 sc in next st] 2 times—6 sts.

Rnds 3, 8: Sc in each st around.

Rnd 4: [Sc in next 2 sts, 2 sc in next st] 2 times—8 sts.

Rnd 5: [Sc in next st, 2 sc in next st] 4 times—12 sts.

Rnd 6: [Sc in next 4 sts, sc2tog] 2 times—10 sts.

Rnd 7: [Sc in next 4 sts, 2 sc in next st] 2 times—12 sts.

Rnd 9: (ankle opening) Sc in next 4 sts, ch 4, sk 4, sc in next 4 sts—12 sts.

Rnd 10: Sc in next 4 sts, sc in next 4 ch, sc in next 4 sts—12 sts. Stuff shoe.

Rnd 11: Sc2tog 6 times—6 sts. Fasten off and close hole in back of shoe.

LEG

Rnd 1: Join A in lower corner of ankle opening at top of shoe with (sl st, ch 1, sc) (counts as 1 sc), sc in next 7 sts around inside of ankle opening—8 sts.

Rnd 2: Sc in each st around.

Rnd 3: 2 FLsc in each st around—16 sts.

Rnd 4: BPsc in each st around.

Rnd 5: [Sc in next 2 sts, sc2tog] 4 times—12 sts.

Rnd 6: Sc in each st around.

Rnd 7: [Sc in next st, sc2tog] 4 times—8 sts.

Rnds 8–13: Sc in each st around. Fasten off.

Heel (make 2)

Row 1: With A, 8 sc in adjustable ring, turn—8 sts.

Row 2: Ch 1, sl st in each st across, fasten off.

Spats (make 2)

With B, leaving a 10–12in/25.4–30.5cm tail, ch 15, join with a sl st to form a ring.

Rnd 1: [Sc in next 3 sts, sc2tog] 3 times—12 sts.

Rnd 2: [Sc in next 2 sts, sc2tog] 3 times—9 sts.

Rnd 3: FLsl st in next 9 sts.

Rnd 4: FPsc in next 9 sts. Fasten off.

With beg tail, draw up a loop in st at base of slip knot, ch 8, fasten off.

With round edge of heel facing back of shoe, sew in place. Slip spat over leg and position around the ankle. Stuff leg. Bring spat strap under foot to opposite side of spat and sew in place.

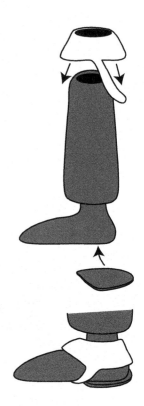

Sew open edge of leg to body.

HAND AND ARM (make 2)

Rnd 1: With C, 6 sc in adjustable ring—6 sts.

Rnd 2: 2 sc in each st around—12 sts.

Rnds 3–4, 10–11, 13–14: Sc in each st around.

Rnds 5, 15: [Sc in next st, sc2tog] 4 times—8 sts.

Rnd 6: Sc in each st around. Stuff hand.

Rnd 7: With B, FPsc in each st around.

Rnd 8: BLsc in each st around.

Rnd 9: 2 FLsc in each st around—16 sts.

Rnd 12: [Sc in next 2 sts, sc2tog] 4 times—12 sts.

Rnd 15: [Sc in next st, sc2tog] 4 times—8 sts.

Rnds 16–19: Sc in each st around. Fasten off. Stuff arm. Flatten seam and sew closed.

FINGERS (make 8)

Rnd 1: With C, 6 sc in adjustable ring—6 sts.

Rnd 2: Sc in each st around. Fasten off. Do not stuff.

Sew fingers to hand and arms to shoulders.

FRANKIE

A work in progress, Frankie was Dr. Frankenstein's favorite pet project to tinker with until the good Doctor met with a rather "unfortunate accident."

SKILL LEVEL
—Intermediate
Height: 7¼in/18.5cm

- - - - - - - - - - - - - - - - - - - -

MATERIALS

- Cascade 220® 3.5oz/100g, 220yds/200m (100% Peruvian Highland Wool)—one each: #8903 Primavera (A), #9637 Lily Pad (B), #8408 Smoke (C), #8505 White (D), #8555 Black (E), #7822 Van Dyke Brown (F), #8509 Grey (G)
- F-5 (3.75mm) crochet hook
- Black felt and light yellow (buttercream) felt [see page 103 for felt templates]
- Fabric glue
- Sewing needle and thread in black

HEAD

Rnd 1: With A, ch 7, sc in 2nd ch from hook and next 4 ch, 5 sc in next ch. Rotate ch so front loops are facing up. FLsc in next 4 sts, 4 sc in next ch—18 sts.

Rnd 2: Sc in next 6 sts, 2 sc in next 3 sts, sc in next 6 sts, 2 sc in next 3 sts—24 sts.

Rnd 3: Hdc in next st, sc in next 5 sts, hdc in next 7 sts, sc in next 5 sts, hdc in next 6 sts—24 sts.

Rnds 4–6, 8–9: Sc in each st around.

Rnd 7: [Sc in next 4 sts, sc2tog] 4 times—20 sts.

Rnd 10: [Sc 8, sc2tog] 2 times—18 sts.

Rnd 11: BLsc in next 4 sts, BLsc2tog 2 times, sc in next 6 sts, BLsc2tog 2 times—14 sts. Stuff lower half of head

Rnd 12: FPsc in next 8 sts, sc in next 6 sts—14 sts.

Rnd 13: [Sc in next st, 2 sc in next st] 7 times—21 sts.

Rnd 14: [Sc in next 2 sts, 2 sc in next st] 7 times—28 sts.

Rnd 15: [Sc in next 5 sts, sc2tog] 4 times—24 sts.

Rnd 16: [BLsc in next st, BLsc2tog] 8 times—16 sts.

Rnd 17: Sc2tog 8 times—8 sts. Fasten off. Stuff head. Flatten seam and sew closed.

BOTTOM LIP

Row 1: Starting on the RS of the line of exposed front lps in Rnd 11, join A with (sl st, ch 1, sc) (counts as 1 sc), FLsc in next 9 sts, turn—10 sts.

Rows 2–3: Ch 1, sc in each st across, turn. Fasten off.

Roll lip toward chin and sew 3rd row to 1st row. Work 1–2 long sts with E from one corner of mouth to the other, secure.

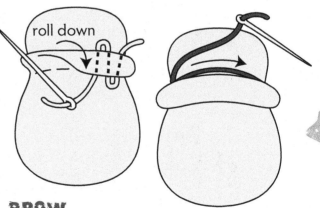

BROW

Rep the bottom lip on the 10 exposed front loops on Rnd 16.

NOSE

Rnd 1: With A, 6 sc in adjustable ring—6 sts.

Rnds 2–3: Sc in each st around. Fasten off. Stuff nose. Sew open edge to face so it rests on bottom lip.

EYES

Cut two eyes from light yellow felt and two pupils from black felt. Assemble eyes and glue or sew to face on either side of nose. With A, work 4–5 satin sts along top of each eye for an eyelid. Push brow detail down in the middle and secure to face with a few sts.

push down

TOOTH

With D, ch 2. Sl st in 2nd ch from hook and fasten off. Tie tails together. Place tooth behind bottom lip and sew in place as illustrated.

EARS (make 2)

Row 1: With A, 4 sc in adjustable ring. Do not join, turn—4 sts.

Row 2: Ch 1, sl st in each st across. Fasten off. Sew ears to sides of head.

HAIR

Rnd 1: With E, 8 sc in adjustable ring—8 sts.

Rnd 2: 2 sc in each st around—16 sts.

Rnd 3: [Sc in next st, 2 sc in next st] 8 times—24 sts.

Rnd 4: [Sl st in next st, ch 2, sl st in base of ch, sl st in next st, ch 3, sl st in base of ch-3] 12 times. Fasten off. With WS facing up, sew hair to top of head.

BODY

Rnd 1: With B, ch 13, sc in 2nd ch from hook and in next 10 ch, 5 sc in next ch. Rotate ch so front loops are facing up. Sc in next 10 ch, 4 FLsc in next ch—30 sts.

Rnd 2: 2 hdc in next st, sc in next 10 sts, 2 hdc in next 5 sts, sc in next 10 sts, 2 hdc in next 4 sts—40 sts.

Rnd 3: BPsc in each st around.

Rnd 4: Sc in each st around.

Rnd 5: [Sc in next 8 sts, sc2tog] 4 times—36 sts.

Rnd 6: (arm opening) Sl st in next 2 sts, sc in next 11 sts, ch 4, sk 6, sc in next 13 sts, ch 4, sk 4—34 sts.

TORSO

Rnd 7: Sk 2, sc in next 11 sts, sc in next 4 ch, sc in next 13 sts, sc in next 4 ch—32 sts.

Rnd 8: [Sc in next 6 sts, sc2tog] 4 times—28 sts.

Rnd 9: [Sc in next 5 sts, sc2tog] 4 times—24 sts.

Rnds 10–17: Sc in each st around.

Rnd 18: With C, [BLsc in next 4 sts, BLsc2tog] 4 times—20 sts.

Rnd 19: Sc in each st around. Stuff body. Fasten off. Flatten bottom and sew closed.

SHIRT EDGE

Rnd 1: With body upside down, join B with (sl st, ch 1, sc) in Rnd 18 (counts as 1 sc), sc in each exposed front loop around—20 sts.

Rnd 2: Sl st in each st around. Fasten off.

ARM (make 2)

Turn body upside down.

Rnd 1: Join B in lower corner of arm opening with (sl st 1, ch 1, sc) (counts as 1 sc), sc next 9 sts around inside of arm opening—10 sts.

Rnds 2–3, 5–7: Sc in each st around.

Rnd 4: [Sc in next 4 sts, 2 sc in next st] 2 times—12 sts.

Rnd 8: [Sc in next 5 sts, 2 sc in next st] 2 times—14 sts.

Rnds 9–11: Sc in each st around. Stuff sleeve.

Rnd 12: BLsc2tog 7 times—7 sts.

HAND

Rnd 13: With A, FPsc in each st around.

Rnd 14: 2 sc in each st around—14 sts.

Rnd 15: Sc in each st around.

Rnd 16: [Sc in next 5 sts, sc2tog] 2 times—12 sts.

Rnds 17–20: Sc in each st around. Fasten off. Lightly stuff hand, flatten seam to run parallel with front of body. Curl hand back to make a fist shape and sew in place. With E, work 2 long stitches over ends of curled portion of hands to define fingers.

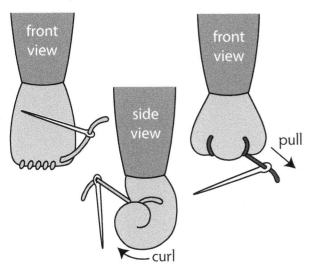

SLEEVE EDGE

Rnd 1: With hand pointed up, join B with (sl st, ch 1, sc) in rnd 12 (counts as 1 sc), sc in each exposed front loop around—14 sts.

Rnd 2: Sl st in each st around. Fasten off. Repeat on other arm.

THUMBS (make 2)

Rnd 1: With A, 6 sc in adjustable ring—6 sts.

Rnd 2: Sc in each st around. Fasten off. Do not stuff.

Attach open edges of thumbs to inside edges of hands.

SHOE AND LEG (make 2)

Rnd 1: With E, 8 sc in adjustable ring—8 sts.

Rnd 2: 2 sc in each st around—16 sts.

Rnds 3, 7: Sc in each st around.

Rnd 4: [Sc in next 7 sts, 2 sc in next st] 2 times—18 sts.

Rnd 5: [Sc in next 7 sts, sc2tog] 2 times—16 sts.

Rnd 6: [Sc in next 2 sts, sc2tog] 4 times—12 sts.

Rnd 8: (ankle opening) Sc in next 4 sts, ch 4, sk 4, sc in next 4 sts—12 sts.

Rnd 9: Sc in next 4 sts, sc in next 4 ch, sc in next 4 sts—12 sts. Stuff shoe.

Rnd 10: Sc2tog 6 times—6 sts. Fasten off and close hole in back of shoe.

LEG

Rnd 1: Join C in stitch of ankle opening at the top of shoe with (sl st, ch 1, 2 sc) (counts as 2 sc), 2 sc in next 7 sts around inside of ankle opening—16 sts.

Rnd 2: BPsc in each st around.

Rnd 3: Sc in each st around.

Rnd 4: [Sc in next 2 sts, sc2tog] 4 times—12 sts.

Rnds 5–7: Sc in each st around. Fasten off. Stuff leg. Sew open edge of leg to body.

SHOE SOLE

Rnd 1: With F, ch 6, sc in 2nd ch from hook and next 3 ch, 5 sc in next ch. Rotate ch so front loops are facing up. Sc in next 3 sts, sc 4 in next ch—16 sts.

Rnd 2: 2 hdc in next st, hdc in next 3 sts, 2 hdc in next 5 sts, hdc in next 3 sts, 2 hdc in next 4 sts—26 sts.

Rnds 3, 6: BPsc in each st around.

Rnds 4–5: Sc in each st around.

Rnd 7: Sc2tog around—13 sts. Fasten off. Stuff sole and seam in a straight line at the top of sole. Sew top of sole to bottom of foot.

BOLTS (make 2)

Note: work sl st as loosely as possible.

Rnd 1: With G, 8 sc in adjustable ring—8 sts.

Rnd 2: BLsl st in each st around.

Rnd 3: [Sk 1, BLsl st in next st] 4 times—4 sts.

Rnds 4–5: Sl st in each st around. Fasten off. Sew open edges of bolts to sides of head close to body.

FINISHING

With E, embroider scars on chin and hand, if desired. To give stitches extra pop, go over black st with gray.

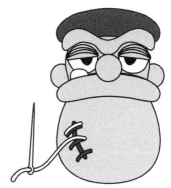

FRANNY

After Dr. Frankenstein met with his rather "unfortunate accident," Franny was compelled to update Frankie to her very own specifications . . . and she now has the perfect man to call her own!

SKILL LEVEL
—Intermediate
Height: 10in/25.5cm, including hair

- -

MATERIALS

- Cascade 220® 3.5oz/100g, 220yds/200m (100% Peruvian Highland Wool)—one each: #9636 Frosty Green (A), #9499 Sand (B), #8010 Natural (C), #9614 Dusk (D), #8505 White (E), #8555 Black (F), #8509 Grey (G), #7822 Van Dyke Brown (H)
- Size F-5 (3.75mm) crochet hook
- White felt [see page 103 for felt templates]
- Black pipe cleaner (1)
- Fabric glue
- Sewing needle and thread

HEAD

Rnd 1: With A, 8 sc in adjustable ring—8 sts.

Rnd 2: 2 sc in each st around—16 sts.

Rnd 3: [Sc in next 3 sts, 2 sc in next st] 4 times—20 sts.

Rnd 4: [Sc in next 4 sts, 2 sc in next st] 4 times—24 sts.

Rnds 5–6, 8, 10, 12–13: Sc in each st around.

Rnd 7: [Sc in next 4 sts, sc2tog] 4 times—20 sts.

Rnd 9: [Sc in next 3 sts, sc2tog] 4 times—16 sts.

Rnd 11: [Sc in next 2 sts, sc2tog] 4 times—12 sts.

Rnd 14: [Sc in next st, sc2tog] 4 times—8 sts. Fasten off. Stuff head, flatten seam and close with mattress stitch.

HAIR

Rnd 1: With F, 8 sc in adjustable ring—8 sts.

Rnd 2: 2 Sc in each st around—16 sts.

Rnd 3: [Sc in next st, 2 sc in next st] 8 times—24 sts.

Rnd 4: [Sc in next 2 sts, 2 sc in next st] 8 times—32 sts.

Rnds 5–9, 11–14, 16: Sc in each st around.

Rnd 10: [Sc in next 6 sts, sc2tog] 4 times—28 sts.

Rnd 15: [Sc in next 5 sts, sc2tog] 4 times—24 sts.

Rnd 17: Sc in next 10 sts, sl st in next 2 sts, (sc, hdc, ch 2, sl st in 2nd ch from hook, sc) in next st, sl st in next 2 st, sc in next 9 sts. Stuff hair. Fasten off. With the widow's peak positioned in front, angle hair back and sew in place, stuff before closing seam.

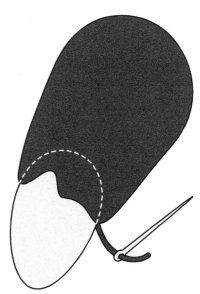

side view

EARS (make 2)

With A, 4 sc in adjustable ring. Do not join. Fasten off. Sew ears to sides of head directly below hair line.

RIGHT WHITE HAIR STRIPE

With E, ch 14, sc in 2nd ch from hook, sc3tog, sc in next ch, 3 sc in next ch, sc in next ch, sc3tog, sc in next ch, 3 sc in next ch, sc in next ch. Fasten off.

LEFT WHITE HAIR STRIPE

With E, ch 14, sc in 2nd ch from hook, 3 sc in next ch, sc in next ch, sc3tog, sc in next ch, 3 sc in next ch, sc in next ch, sc3tog, sc in next ch. Fasten off.

Sew stripes above the ears.

NOSE

With A, 4 sc in adjustable ring, sl st to join. Fasten off. Sew edge to center of face.

GOGGLES (make 2)

Rnd 1: With F, 6 sc in adjustable ring.

Rnd 2: [BLsc in next 2 sts, 2 BLsc in next st] 2 times—8 sts.

Rnd 3: With G, BPsc in each st around. Fasten off. Invert goggle so Rnd 3 sts are facing out. Sew goggles to face on either side of nose. Cut 2 white felt circles, glue to Rnd 3 rim of goggles. With H, embroider short sts bet goggles for nose bridge, work long sts from outside edges to create a strap around head.

invert

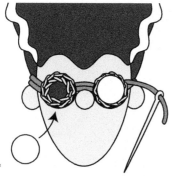

BODY

Rnd 1: With C, 8 sc in adjustable ring—8 sts.

Rnd 2: 2 sc in each st around—16 sts.

Rnd 3: [Sc in next st, 2 sc in next st] 8 times—24 sts.

Rnd 4: [Sc in next 5 sts, 2 sc in next st] 4 times—28 sts.

Rnd 5: FPsc in each st around.

Rnd 6: [BLsc in next 5 sts, BLsc2tog] 4 times—24 sts.

Rnds 7–8, 10, 12–13: Sc in each st around.

Rnd 9: [Sc in next 4 sts, sc2tog] 4 times—20 sts.

Rnd 11: [Sc in next 3 sts, sc2tog] 4 times—16 sts.

Rnd 14: [Sc in next 2 sts, sc2tog] 4 times—12 sts.

Rnd 15: With B, [BLsc in next st, BLsc2tog] 4 times—8 sts.

Rnd 16: Sc in next 3 sts, sl st in next 2 sts, sc in next 3 sts. Stuff body.

Rnds 17–18: Sc in next 2 sts, sl st in next 4 sts, sc in next 2 sts. Fasten off. Stuff neck. The head may be heavy, insert a looped piece of pipe cleaner into the body to support the head and neck.

SKIRT

Rnd 1: With body upside down, join C to Rnd 5 with (sl st, ch 1, sc) (counts as 1 sc), sc in each exposed front loop around—28 sts.

Rnds 2–5: Sc in each st around. Fasten off.

NECK EDGE

Rnd 1: With body upside down, join C in Rnd 15 with (sl st, ch 1) (counts as sl st), sc 2tag, (sc in next lp, sc 2tog) 3 times—8 sts. Fasten off.

Sew open edge of neck to head behind chin (the sl sts should line up under the chin). Wrap yarn tail around neck and secure at base of neck behind head. Tack chin down to base of neck.

HAND AND ARM

Rnd 1: With A, 6 sc in adjustable ring—6 sts.

Rnd 2: 2 sc in each st around—12 sts.

Rnds 3–4: Sc in each st around.

Rnd 5: [Sc in next st, sc2tog] 4 times—8 sts. Stuff hand.

Rnd 6: [Sc in next 2 sts, sc2tog] 2 times—6 sts.

Rnd 7: With B, FPsc in each st around.

Rnds 8–10: BLsc in each st around.

Rnds 11–12: BLhdc in next 2 sts, BLsl st in next 3 sts, BLhdc in next st. Stuff lower arm.

Rnds 13–15: BLsc in each st around. Stuff upper arm and fasten off. Sew to shoulder with elbows pointed back.

FINGERS (make 8)

Rnd 1: With A, 6 sc in adjustable ring—6 sts.

Rnd 2: Sc in each st around. Fasten off. Do not stuff. Taking note of elbow shaping, sew open edges of 4 fingers to front edge of each hand.

BOOT AND LEG (make 2)

Rnd 1: With F, 8 sc in adjustable ring—8 sts.

Rnd 2: 2 sc in each st around—16 sts.

Rnds 3, 7: Sc in each st around.

Rnd 4: [Sc in next 7 sts, 2 sc in next st] 2 times—18 sts.

Rnd 5: [Sc in next 7 sts, sc2tog] 2 times—16 sts.

Rnd 6: [Sc in next 2 sts, sc2tog] 4 times—12 sts.

Rnd 8: (ankle opening) Sc in next 4 sts, ch 4, sk 4, sc in next 4 sts—12 sts.

Rnd 9: Sc in next 4 sts, sc in next 4 ch, sc in next 4 sts—12 sts. Stuff boot.

Rnd 10: Sc2tog 6 times—6 sts. Fasten off and close hole in back of shoe.

LEG

Rnd 1: Join F in ankle opening at the top of boot with (sl st, ch 1, sc) (counts as sc), sc in next 7 sts around inside of ankle opening—8 sts.

Rnds 2–4: Sc in each st around.

Rnd 5: FPsc in each st around.

Rnd 6: With B, [BLsc in next 2 sts, BLsc2tog] 2 times—6 sts.

Rnds 7–8: BLsc in each st around.

Rnd 9: [BLsc in next 2 sts, 2 BLsc in next st] 2 times—8 sts. Stuff leg. Fasten off.

BOOT CUFF

Rnd 1: With foot pointed down, join F to exposed front lps of Rnd 5 with (sl st, ch 1, sc) (counts as first sc), work 7 sc into exposed front lps of Rnd 5—8 sts. Fasten off.

HEEL (make 2)

Row 1: With F, 8 sc in adjustable ring, turn—8 sts.

Row 2: Ch 1, sc in each st across. Fasten off. With round edge of heel facing back of boot, sew in place.

Sew open edges of legs to bottom of body.

LAB APRON

Row 1: With F, ch 13, sc 2nd ch from hook and next 11 ch, turn—12sts.

Rows 2–8, 10–12: Ch 1, sc in each st across, turn.

Row 9: Ch 1, sc2tog, sc in next 8 sts, sc2tog, turn—10 sts.

Row 13: Ch 1, sc2tog, sc in next 6 sts, sc2tog, turn—8 sts.

Row 14: Ch 1, sc2tog, sc in next 4 sts, sc2tog, ch 15, sl st in 2nd ch from hook and next 13 ch, fasten off. Join F on opposite corner of Row 14, ch 15, sl st in 2nd ch from hook and next 13 ch, fasten off.

APRON TIES

Join F to side edge in middle of apron, ch 15, sl st in 2nd ch from hook and next 13 sts, fasten off. Rep on opposite edge.

Attach apron by tying the apron ties behind the neck and waist.

FINISHING

With D, embroider 3 lazy daisy stitches in a "Y" shape on lower half of face for lips. Rep to thicken the lips. With F, work a short stitch across center of lips to create a mouth line.

CARL OF THE DEAD

Carl was sure that he had left his arm on his end table when he came home from a long day of terrorizing the living. Where could it be?

SKILL LEVEL
—Intermediate
Height: 8½in/21.5cm

- -

MATERIALS

- Knit Picks® Wool of the Andes 1.8oz/50g, 110yds/101m (100% Peruvian Highland Wool)—one each: #24074 Pampas Heather (A), #25070 Cadet (B), #25067 Blossom Heather (C), #25985 Brown Sugar (D), #25980 Victorian (E), #23420 Coal (F), #23432 Cloud (G)

- F-5 (3.75mm) crochet hook

- Yellow (sunshine) felt [see page 103 for felt templates]

- Fabric glue

- Sewing needle and thread in black

HEAD

Rnd 1: With A, 8 sc in adjustable ring—8 sts.

Rnd 2: 2 sc in each st around—16 sts.

Rnd 3: [Sc in next 3 sts, 2 sc in next st] 4 times—20 sts.

Rnd 4: [Sc in next 4 sts, 2 sc in next st] 4 times—24 sts.

Rnds 5–6, 10–11: Sc in each st around.

Rnd 7: Sc in next 4 sts, [sc in next st, sc2tog, sc in next st] 4 times, sc in next 4 sts—20 sts.

Rnd 8: Sc in next 4 sts, BPsc in next 12 sts, sc in next 4 sts—20 sts.

Rnd 9: [Sc in next 3 sts, sc2tog] 4 times—16 sts.

Rnd 12: Sc in next 4 sts, hdc in next 8 sts, sc in next 4 sts.

Rnd 13: Sc2tog, sl st in next st, ch 3, sl st in base of ch-3, sc2tog, sl st in next st, ch 3, sl st in base of ch-3, sl st in next st, ch 2, sl st in base of ch-2, sc2tog, sl st in next st, ch 2, sl st in base of ch-2, sl st in next 2 sts, ch 3, sl st in base of ch-3, sc2tog, sl st in next st, ch 2, sl st in base of ch-2, sl st in next st. Fasten off.

Lip Row 1: Join A, FLsl st in 12 exposed loops of Rnd 8. Fasten off.

With B, embroider a long st from one corner of the mouth to the other, then back through the head to the first corner again. Pull gently to shape jaw line. Work 2 short sts in the middle of the face for nostrils.

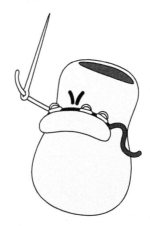

With G, work 3 French knots on mouth for teeth.

EYE BASE SMALL

Rnd 1: With D, 4 sc in adjustable ring—4 sts.

Rnd 2: [Sc in next st, 2 sc in next st] 2 times—6 sts. Fasten off.

EYE BASE LARGE

Rnd 1: With D, 6 sc in adjustable ring—6 sts.

Rnd 2: [Sc in next 2 sts, 2 sc in next st] 2 times—8 sts. Fasten off.

Sew eyes to the front of the face with 4–5 sts bet them. Cut two eyes from light yellow felt. Using black sewing thread, embroider two small pupils on each eye. Glue or sew to eye bases.

BRAAAINNNNNNSSSSS!

Rnd 1: With C, 8 sc in adjustable ring—8 sts.

Rnd 2: 2 sc in each st around—16 sts.

Rnd 3: Sc in each st around.

Rnd 4: Sc2tog 8 times—8 sts. Stuff brain.

Rnd 5: [Sc in next 2 sts, sc2tog] 2 times—6 sts. Fasten off. Close hole at bottom of brain. With E, work a tight twisty line of sc or embroidered ch sts on surface of brain. Work a long stitch with C around brain and pull tightly to separate the two hemispheres.

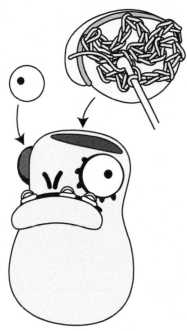

Stuff head, leaving room for brain. Insert brain into top of head and use A to secure with a few stitches.

EARS AND LARGE EYELID (make 3)

Row 1: With A, 6 sc in adjustable ring. Do not join. turn—6 sts.

Row 2: Ch 1, sl st in each st across. Fasten off.

SMALL EYELID

With A, 4 sc in adjustable ring. Do not join. Fasten off.

Sew ears to sides of head. Sew flat edge of eyelids above eye so they flare out.

BODY

Rnd 1: With B, 8 sc in adjustable ring—8 sts.

Rnd 2: 2 sc in each st around—16 sts.

Rnds 3, 5, 9, 15, 18: Sc in each st around.

Rnd 4: [Sc in next 3 sts, 2 sc in next st] 4 times—20 sts.

Rnd 6: [Sc in next 4 sts, 2 sc in next st] 4 times—24 sts.

Rnd 7: With G, FPsc in each st around.

Rnd 8: BLsc in each st around.

Rnd 10: [Sc in next 4 sts, sc2tog] 5 times—20 sts.

Rnds 11–12: Hdc in next 5 sts, sc in next 10 sts, hdc in next 5 sts.

Rnd 13: Hdc in next 5 sts, sl st in next 10 sts, hdc in next 5 sts.

Rnd 14: [Sc in next 3 sts, sc2tog] 4 times—16 sts.

Rnd 16: [Sc in next 2 sts, sc2tog] 4 times—12 sts. Stuff body.

Rnd 17: With A, BLsc in each st around.

Rnd 19: [Sc in next 4 sts, sc2tog] 2 times—10 sts.

Rnds 20–21: Sc in each st around. Fasten off. Stuff neck. With the hdc of Rnds 11–13 in the back, sew open edge of neck to back of head.

NECK EDGE DETAIL

With G, sc in the 12 exposed front loops in Rnd 17. Fasten off.

TATTERED SHIRT EDGE DETAIL

Rnd 1: Holding body upside down, join G to FPsc lps of Rnd 7 with (sl st, ch 1, sc) (counts as 1 sc), sc in next 23 FPsc of Rnd 7—24 sts.

Rnd 2: [Sl st in next 2 sts, ch 2, sl st in base of ch-2] 2 times, sl st in next st, ch 3, sl st in base of ch-3, sl st in next st, [sl st in next 2 sts, ch 2, sl st in base of ch-2] 2 times, sl st in next st, ch 3, sl st in base of ch-3, [sl st in next 4 sts, ch 2, sl st in base of ch-2, sl st in next 2 sts, ch 3, sl st in base of ch-3] 2 times. Sl st in next ch. Fasten off.

SLEEVES (make 2)

Rnd 1: With G, 4 sc in adjustable ring—4 sts.

Rnd 2: 2 Sc in each st around—8 sts.

Rnds 3–5: Sc in each st around.

Rnd 6: Sl st in next st, ch 3, sl st in base of ch-3, sl st in next st, ch 2, sl st in base of ch-2, sl st in next st, [sl st in next 2 sts, ch 2, sl st in base of ch-2] 2 times, sl st in next st. Fasten off.

HAND AND ARM

Rnd 1: With A, 6 sc in adjustable ring—6 sts.

Rnd 2: 2 sc in each st around—12 sts.

Rnds 3–4, 7–10: Sc in each st around.

Rnd 5: [Sc in next st, sc2tog] 4 times—8 sts. Stuff hand.

Rnd 6: [Sc in next 2 sts, sc2tog] 2 times—6 sts.

Rnds 11–12: Hdc in next 2 sts, sl st in next 3 sts, hdc in next st. Stuff lower arm.

Rnds 13–15: Sc in each st around. Stuff upper arm and fasten off.

Insert arm into sleeve and secure with a few stitches. Sew sleeve to shoulder of body. Take notice of elbow shaping on full arm.

ARM STUB

Rnd 1: With C, 6 sc in adjustable ring—6 sts.

Rnds 2–3: With A, BLsc in each st around.

Rnds 4–6: Sc in each st around.

Stuff arm stub and fasten off. Close hole at top of arm stub. With G, work a chunky French knot in the middle of Rnd 1 for a bone. Insert arm stub into sleeve and secure with a few sts. Sew sleeve to shoulder of body.

DE-ATTACHED HAND AND ARM

Work as for **Hand and Arm** to Rnd 10.

Rnd 11: [Sc in next 2 sts, 2 sc in next st] 2 times—8 sts. Stuff arm.

Rnd 12: With C, [BLsc in next 2 sts, BLsc2tog] 2 times—6 sts. Fasten off. Add more stuffing before closing hole.

Option 1: With G, work a chunky French knot in middle of Rnd 12 for a bone. Keep arm separate from body to put in Daisy the Zombie Dog's (page 79) mouth.

Option 2: With G, work 1 or 2 sts to attach the middle of Rnd 12 to the bone detail on the arm stub and allow the arm to hang.

LEG AND FOOT (make 2)

Rnd 1: With A, 8 sc in adjustable ring—8 sts.

Rnd 2: 2 sc in each st around—16 sts.

Rnd 3: (foot opening) Sc in next 2 sts, sc2tog, sc in next st, ch 6, sk 6, sc in next st, sc2tog, sc in next 2 sts—14 sts.

Rnd 4: Sc2tog, sc in next 2 sts, sc in next 6 ch, sc in next 2 sts, sc2tog—12 sts.

Rnd 5: [Sc in next st, sc2tog] 4 times—8 sts.

Rnds 6–9: Sc in each st around.

Rnd 10: With B, [FLsc in next st, 2 FLsc in next st] 4 times—12 sts.

Rnd 11: [BLsc in next 4 sts, BLsc2tog] 2 times—10 sts.

Rnds 12–16: Sc in each st around. Fasten off.

FOOT

Rnd 1: Working into foot opening, join A with (sl st, ch 1, sc) in same st (counts as 1 sc), sc in next 11 sts around inside of foot opening—12 sts.

Rnds 2–3: Sc in each st around.

Rnd 4: [Sc in next 2 sts, 2 sc in next st] 4 times—16 sts.

Rnd 5: Sc in each st around. Fasten off. Stuff foot, flatten and whip stitch toe edge closed. Stuff leg.

TATTERED PANT EDGE

Rnd 1: With foot facing up, join B to exposed front lps of Rnd 10 with (sl st, ch 1, sc) in same st (counts as 1 sc), sc in next 11 exposed front loops of Rnd 10—12 sts.

Rnd 2: Sl st in next 2 sts, *ch 2, sl st in base of ch-2, sl st in next 2 sts, ch 3, sl st in base of ch-3, sl st in next st, ch 2, sl st in base of ch-2**, sl st in next 3 sts, rep from * to **, sl st in next st. Fasten off. Sew open edges of legs to hips. Add more stuffing before closing seam, if needed.

FINGERS AND BIG TOE (make 10)

Rnd 1: With A, 6 sc in adjustable ring—6 sts.

Rnd 2: Sc in each st around. Fasten off. Do not stuff.

Sew open edges of 4 fingers to front edge of each hand and 1 big toe to each foot.

FINISHING

With F, work 3 long sts to define the toes.

DAISY THE ZOMBIE DOG

Daisy is super-excited about burying the bone she found on Carl's end table this evening. It's a really nice bone too, since it still has some fingers attached. Before she buries it, perhaps Carl would like to play a game of fetch first?

SKILL LEVEL
—Intermediate

Height: 5in/12.75cm

- - - - - - - - - - - - - - - - - - - -

MATERIALS

- Knit Picks® Wool of the Andes 1.8oz/50g, 110yds/101m (100% Peruvian Highland Wool)— one each: #25645 Opal Heather (A), #25985 Brown Sugar (B), #25980 Victorian (C), #23420 Coal (D), #23432 Cloud (E)

- F-5 (3.75mm) crochet hook

- Yellow (sunshine) felt and black felt [see page 103 for felt templates]

- Fabric glue

- Sewing needle and thread in black

HEAD

Rnd 1: With A, ch 4, sc in 2nd ch from hook and next st, 4 sc in next st. Rotate ch so front loops are facing up. Sc in next st, 3 sc in next st—10 sts.

Rnd 2: [Sc in next 4 sts, 2 sc in next st] 2 times—12 sts.

Rnd 3: Sc2tog 6 times—6 sts.

Rnds 4–5: Sc in each st around. Stuff muzzle.

Rnd 6: [Sc in next 2 sts, 2 sc in next st] 2 times—8 sts.

Rnd 7: [Sc in next 3 sts, 2 sc in next st] 2 times—10 sts.

Rnd 8: [Sc in next 4 sts, 2 sc in next st] 2 times—12 sts.

Rnd 9: [Sc in next st, 2 sc in next st] 6 times—18 sts.

Rnd 10: [Sc in next 2 sts, 2 sc in next st] 6 times—24 sts.

Rnd 11: Sc in each st around.

Rnd 12: [Sc in next 4 sts, sc2tog] 4 times—20 sts.

Rnd 13: [Sc in next 3 sts, sc2tog] 4 times—16 sts.

Rnd 14: [Sc in next 2 sts, sc2tog] 4 times—12 sts. Stuff head.

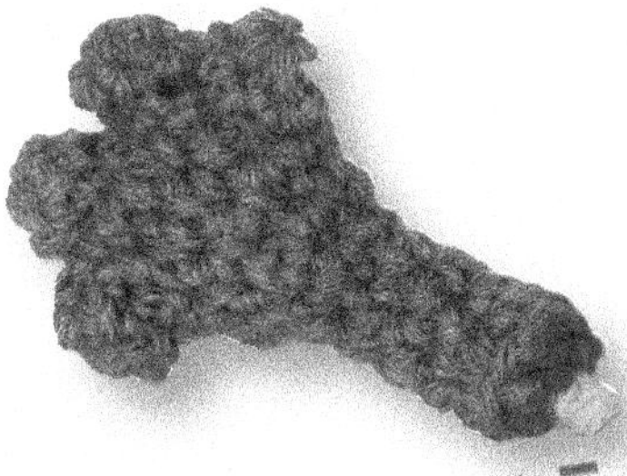

Rnd 15: [Sc in next st, sc2tog] 4 times—8 sts. Fasten off and close hole.

Attach 1 piece of A through top of head for a fringe of hair (see page 21).

CHIN

Rnds 1–3: Rep Rnds 1–3 of head.

Rnds 4–6: Sc in each st around. Fasten off, stuff lightly. Make sure the front of the chin and muzzle are parallel to each other before sewing open edge of chin to the head. Add a nose bridge detail by pinching the material above muzzle to create a ridge roughly 3 rnds tall. Work a running stitch back and forth through the sides of the ridge to hold shaping in place.

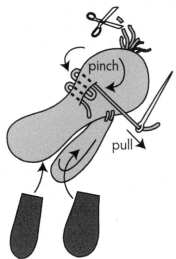

Cut a top and bottom jaw shape from black felt and glue or sew to the inside of the chin and muzzle.

NOSE

Rnd 1: With D, 6 sc in adjustable ring—6 sts.

Rnd 2: [Sc in next st, sc2tog] 2 times—4 sts. Fasten off.

Sew open edge of nose to front of muzzle. Using tail, work 1–2 long sts down front of muzzle and pull tightly to shape lip cleft.

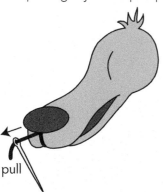

FULL EAR

Rnd 1: With B, ch 5, sc in 2nd ch from hook and next 2 sts, 5 hdc in next st. Rotate ch so front loops are facing up. Sc in next 2 sts, 2 sc in next st—12 sts. Fasten off.

HALF EAR

Row 1: With B, 3 sc in adjustable ring. Do not join, turn—3 sts.

Row 2: Ch 1, sl st in next st, ch 2, sl st in base of ch-2, sl st in next st, ch 3, sl st in base of ch-3, sl st in next st, ch 2, sl st in base of ch-2. Fasten off. Attach ears to sides of head.

EYE BASE (make 2)

Rnd 1: With B, 4 sc in adjustable ring—4 sts.

Rnd 2: [Sc in next st, 2 sc in next st] 2 times—6 sts. Fasten off.

Sew open edges of eye bases to head on either side of nose bridge shaping.

Cut two eyes from light yellow felt. Using black sewing thread, embroider two small pupils in each eye. Glue or sew to eye bases.

BODY

Rnd 1: With A, 8 sc in adjustable ring—8 sts.

Rnd 2: [Sc in next st, 2 sc in next st] 4 times—12 sts.

Rnd 3: [Sc in next 2 sts, 2 sc in next st] 4 times—16 sts.

Rnd 4: (neck opening) Sc in next 6 sts, ch-4, sk 4, sc in next 6 sts—16 sts.

Rnd 5: Sc in next 6 sts, sc in next 4 ch, sc in next 6 sts.

Rnd 6: [Sc in next 6 sts, sc2tog] 2 times—14 sts.

Rnd 7: With C, [BLsc in next 5 sts, BLsc2tog] 2 times—12 sts.

Rnds 8–11: Sc in each st around.

Rnd 12: With A, [FLsc in next 2 sts, 2 FLsc in next st] 4 times—16 sts.

Rnd 13: BLsc in each st around.

Rnd 14: [Sc in next 6 sts, sc2tog] 2 times—14 sts.

Rnd 15: [Sc in next 5 sts, sc2tog] 2 times—12 sts.

Rnd 16: [Sc in next st, sc2tog] 4 times—8 sts. Fasten off. Stuff and close hole in back of body.

NECK

Rnd 1: Starting in neck opening, join A with (sl st, ch 1) in same st (counts as 1 sc), sc in next 7 sts around inside of neck opening—8 sts.

Rnds 2–3: Sc in each st around. Fasten off. Stuff neck.

TATTERED FRONT TORSO EDGE

With back of torso facing up, join A to exposed lp of Rnd 6 with (sl st, ch 1) in same st (counts as 1 sl st), sl st in next st, *ch 2, sl st in base of ch-2, **sl st in next 2 sts, ch 3, sl st in base of ch-3, sl st in next st, ch 2, sl st in base of ch-2***, sl st in next 3 sts. Rep from * to ***, rep from ** to ***. Fasten off.

TATTERED REAR TORSO EDGE

With front of torso facing up, join A to exposed lp of Rnd 12 with (sl st, ch 1) in same st (counts as 1 sl st), sl st in next st, *ch 2, sl st in base of ch-2, sl st st in next 2 sts, ch 3, sl st in base of ch-3, sl st in next st, ch 2, sl st in base of ch-2, sl st in next 3 sts.** Rep from * to **, ch 3, sl st in base of ch-3, sl st in next 2 sts, ch 2, sl st in base of ch-2. Fasten off.

SPINE

With E, ch 7, starting in 2nd ch from hook [sl st in next 2 st, ch 2, sl st in base of ch-2] 3 times.

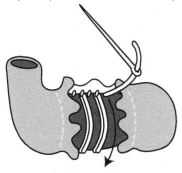

Fasten off. Sew spine down center of Rnds 7–11 of body. Using a double strand of E, embroider 3 ribs on each side same section of body.

LEGS (make 2)

Rnd 1: With A, 8 sc in adjustable ring—8 sts.

Rnd 2: BLsc in next 2 sts, BLhdc in next 4 sts, BLsc in next 2 sts.

Rnd 3: Sl st in next 2 sts, sc in next 4 sts, sl st in next 2 sts—8 sts.

Rnd 4: Sc in next 2 sts, sc2tog 2 times, sc in next 2 sts—6 sts. Stuff foot.

Rnds 5–9: Sc in each st around.

Rnd 10: [Sc in next st, 2 sc in next st] 3 times—9 sts.

LEFT SIDE LEGS ONLY

Rnd 11: Sc in next 4 sts, hdc in next 3 sts, sl st in next 2 sts.

RIGHT SIDE LEGS ONLY

Rnd 11: Hdc in next 2 sts, sc in next 4 sts, sl st in next 2 sts, hdc in next st.

Stuff leg. Sew open edges of legs to body with hdc on Rnd 11 attached directly to shoulders and hips keeping toe shaping on Rnd 1 facing forward. Add more stuffing if needed before closing seam.

FINISHING

Attach a 6in/15cm piece of B in an inconspicuous spot under the belly and draw one tail out through the back of body for tail. Weave in unused tail. Trim tail to 2in/5cm and coat with craft glue. As glue begins to set and becomes less tacky, shape and crimp tail. Trim tail to desired final length.

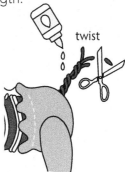

twist

To add a tongue, make one "Full Ear" with C and attach to back of mouth.

MR. HYDE

DR. JEKYLL

DR. JEKYLL AND MR. HYDE

A two-faced kind of guy, Dr. Jekyll and his alter ego, Mr. Hyde, can never agree on the simplest things. One wants to have a nice lunch, the other wants to see a horror film. One wants to take a stroll at the park, the other wants to go to a graveyard party. It's truly about the art of compromise with this duo.

SKILL LEVEL
—Advanced
Height: 10¾in/27.25cm, including hat

- -

MATERIALS

- Knit Picks® Wool of the Andes 1.8oz/50g, 110yds/101m (100% Peruvian Highland Wool)—one each: #24652 Bittersweet Heather (A), #25976 Marble Heather (B), #25633 Garnet Heather (C), #24649 Oyster Heather (D), #24277 Fedora (E), #23420 Coal (F), #23432 Cloud (G)

- F-5 (3.75mm) crochet hook

- Red (big apple) felt, gray (stone) felt, black felt, white felt, and light yellow (buttercream) felt [see page 103 for felt templates]

- Sewing needle and thread in black

- Fiberfill stuffing

- Scissors

- Tapestry needle

- ½in/1cm plastic shank buttons (2) (optional)

BODY

Rnd 1: With A, ch 9, sc in 2nd ch from hook and next 6 sc, 5 sc in next ch. Rotate ch so front loops are facing up. FLsc in next 6 ch, 4 FLsc in next ch—22 sts.

Rnds 2–5, 8–12, 16: Sc in each st around.

Rnd 6: [Sc in next 9 sts, sc2tog] 2 times—20 sts.

Rnd 7: [Sc in next 3 sts, sc2tog] 4 times—16 sts.

Rnd 13: [Sc in next 3 sts, 2 sc in next st] 4 times—20 sts.

Rnd 14: With B, BLsc in each st around.

Rnd 15: [Sc in next 3 sts,sc2tog] 4 times—16 sts.

Rnd 17: [Sc in next 2 sts, sc2tog] 4 times—12 sts. Stuff body firmly.

Rnd 18: Sc2tog 6 times. Fasten off and close hole.

NECK AND TIE

Rnd 1: With C, 4 sc in adjustable ring—4 sts.

Rnd 2: 2 sc in each st around—8 sts.

Rnd 3: BLsc in each st around.

Rnd 4: [Sc in next 3 sts, 2 sc in next st] 2 times—10 sts.

NOTE: You will make one creature for this project: the head, which will turn around, has a face on each side.

Rnd 5: Sl st in next 5 sts, ch 2 (hdc, dc, 2 tr, dc, hdc, ch 2, sl st) in st at base of ch-2, sl st in next 5 sts. Fasten off. Sew open edge of neck to top of body bet shoulders, taking care to leave the tie loose in front. Stuff neck before closing seam.

JACKET COLLAR

Row 1: With A, ch 19, sl st in 2nd ch from hook, sc in next 2 ch, 2 hdc in next ch, ch 1, sl st in next ch, 2 hdc in next ch, hdc in next 6 ch, 2 hdc in next ch, sl st in next ch, ch 1, 2 hdc in next ch, sc in next 2 sts, sl st in next st. Fasten off. Drape collar under scarf and tie overlapping the lapels in the front. Sew inside edges in place. Sc a line of surface sts from bottom edge to the lapels to define the jacket panels.

Using template, cut 3 buttons from gray felt and attach them to the side of the line of sc on front of jacket.

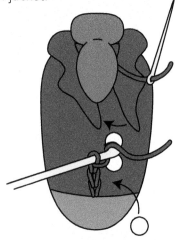

HEAD

Rnd 1: With D, 8 sc in adjustable ring—8 sts.

Rnd 2: 2 Sc in each st around—16 sts.

Rnd 3: [Sc in next st, 2 sc in next st] 8 times—24 sts.

Rnd 4: [Sc in next 2 sts, 2 sc in next st] 8 times—32 sts.

Rnds 5–7, 11–14: Sc in each st around.

Rnd 8: [Sc in next 6 sts, sc2tog] 4 times—28 sts.

Rnd 9: [Sc in next 5 sts, sc2tog] 4 times—24 sts.

Rnd 10: [Sc in next 4 sts, sc2tog] 4 times—20 sts.

Rnd 15: [Sc in next 4 sts, 2 sc in next st] 4 times—24 sts.

Rnd 16: [Sc in next st, sc2tog] 8 times—16 sts.

Thread shank button and yarn tails out through the bottom of the head. Stuff head firmly.

Rnd 17: Sc2tog 8 times—8 sts.

Rnd 18: Sc2tog 4 times—4 sts. Fasten off.

NOSE (make 2)

Rnd 1: With D, 6 sc in adjustable ring—6 sts.

Rnd 2: Sc in each st around. Fasten off.

Sew open edge of nose to center of face. Work chunky French knots (see page 20) on each side of nose. Add a nose bridge detail by pinching the material above the nose to create a ridge roughly 3 rnds tall. Work running sts back and forth through the sides of the ridge to hold the shaping in place. Repeat on the other side of the head.

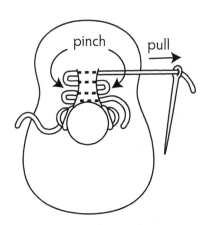

pinch   pull

EARS (make 2)

Row 1: With D, 8 sc in adjustable ring. Do not join, turn—8 sts.

Row 2: Ch 1, sl st in each st across. Fasten off. Attach ears to sides of head.

EYEBROW RIDGE (make 2)

Row 1: With D, ch 11, sc in 2nd ch from hook and in each ch across, turn—10 sts.

Row 2: Ch 1, sc in each st across, turn.

Row 3: Fold piece to match first and last rows, ch 1, sl st in each st across working through both layers at the same time—10 sts. Fasten off.

Dr. Jekyll Eyes: Cut two eyes from white felt and two pupils from black felt. Assemble eyes and glue or sew to face. With D, work 3–4 long satin sts across top edge of each eye for eyelids.

Mr. Hyde Eyes: Cut two eyes from light yellow felt and two pupils from red felt. Make a hole in the center of each red pupil with a sewing needle, then enlarge the hole with a tapestry needle. Glue or sew pupils to yellow eyes. With black thread, work a few stitches into the hole at the center of the red pupil to darken it. Glue or sew the eyes to the face.

Dr. Jekyll Brow: Place brow against head with Row 3 at the bottom. Attach brow in an upside down "U"shape across the forehead using the mattress stitch on the bottom edge and a running stitch on the top edge.

With E, embroider eyebrows as illustrated.

Mr. Hyde Brow: Place brow against head with Row 3 at the top. Attach brow in a "U" shape across the forehead. The bottom of the "U" will be 1–2 rnds above the top of the nose. Sew the bottom edge with the mattress stitch and the top edge with a running stitch. Work a few sts bet center of brow and nose. Pull firmly to draw brow and nose together.

push down

Hyde face

With E, embroider eyebrows and work 1 long st across bottom edge of Dr. Jekyll's eyelids for an eyelash detail.

With F, embroider a simple mouth for Dr. Jekyll and add 2 small satin stitches to each nostril. Cut one mouth shape from black felt and attach to lower part of Mr. Hyde's face. Backstitch a wide crooked smile onto Mr. Hyde's face, working around the top and bottom edges of the mouth shape. With G, work 3–4 sts over the front of the mouth shape to create teeth.

Jekyll face

felt

Hyde face

TOP HAT

Rnd 1: With F, 8 sc in adjustable ring—8 sts.

Rnd 2: 2 sc in each st around—16 sts.

Rnd 3: [Sc in next st, 2 sc in next st] 8 times—24 sts.

Rnd 4: [Sc in next 2 sts, 2 sc in next st] 8 times—32 sts.

Rnd 5: [Sc in next 3 sts, 2 sc in next st] 8 times—40 sts.

Rnd 6: Loosely BLsl st in each st around.

Rnd 7: [BLsc in next 3 sts, BLsc2tog] 8 times—32 sts.

Rnd 8: [Sc in next 2 sts, sc2tog] 8 times—24 sts.

Rnd 9: [Sc in next st, sc2tog] 8 times—16 sts.

Rnd 10: FLsc in each st around.

Rnds 11–12, 14–15: Sc in each st around.

Rnd 13: [Sc in next 3 sts, 2 sc in next st] 4 times—20 sts.

Rnd 16: [Sc in next 4 sts, 2 sc in next st] 4 times—24 sts.

Rnd 17: [BLsc in next 4 sts, BLsc2tog] 4 times—20 sts.

Thread shank button and yarn tails through bottom of hat. With tapestry needle and F, sew Rnd 8 to Rnd 1 to keep brim flat.

Rnd 18: Sc2tog 10 times—10 sts. Fasten off, stuff hat, close hole at top of hat.

Cut 25 8in/20 cm pieces of E and attach them to the back half of Rnd 2 and Rnd 1 of hat brim using the fringe technique. Use a tapestry needle to separate the yarn plies.

With a tapestry needle, draw the two yarn tails from shank button at the bottom of the hat through the head from top to bottom. Pull firmly, secure tails to bottom of head and weave in ends. Draw each yarn tail shank button at the bottom of the head down through the neck and body. Draw each yarn tail out at the location where the leg will be attached to the bottom of the body. Pull yarn firmly and secure. The secure points will be hidden when the legs are installed.

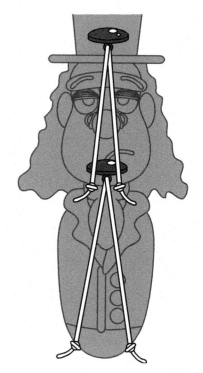

SHOE (make 2)

Rnd 1: With F, 8 sc in adjustable ring—8 sts.

Rnd 2: 2 sc in each st around—16 sts.

Rnds 3, 7: Sc in each st around.

Rnd 4: [Sc in next 7 sts, 2 sc in next st] 2 times—18 sts.

Rnd 5: [Sc in next 7 sts, sc2tog] 2 times—16 sts.

Rnd 6: [Sc in next 2 sts, sc2tog] 4 times—12 sts.

Rnd 8: (ankle opening) Sc in next 4 sts, ch 4, sk 4, sc in next 4 sts—12 sts.

Rnd 9: Sc in next 4 sts, sc in next 4 ch, sc in next 4 sts—12 sts. Stuff shoe.

Rnd 10: Sc2tog 6 times—6 sts. Fasten off and close hole in back of shoe.

LEG (make 2)

Rnd 1: Join B in ankle opening at the top of the shoe with (sl st, ch 1, 2 sc) (counts as 2 sc), 2 sc in next 7 sts around inside of ankle opening—16 sts.

Rnd 2: BPsc in each st around.

Rnds 3, 5–8: Sc in each st around.

Rnd 4: [Sc in next 2 sts, sc2tog] 4 times—12 sts.

Rnd 9: [Sc in next 2 sts, sc2tog] 3 times—9 sts.

Rnds 10–12: Sc in each st around. Fasten off, stuff leg.

Sew open edge of leg to body, covering any connection points from when the head was attached.

HAND AND ARM (make 2)

Rnd 1: With G, 6 sc in adjustable ring– 6 sts.

Rnd 2: 2 sc in each st around—12 sts.

Rnds 3–4, 9–11: Sc in each st around.

Rnd 5: [Sc in next st, sc2tog] 4 times—8 sts.

Rnd 6: Sc in each st around. Stuff hand.

Rnd 7: With A, [FLsc in next st, 2 FLsc in next st] 4 times—12 sts.

Rnd 8: BPsc in each st around.

Rnd 12: [Sc in next st, sc2tog] 4 times—8 sts.

Rnds 13–16: Sc in each st around. Fasten off. Stuff arm. Flatten seam and sew closed.

(Optional jointed arms) Before sewing arms closed, tie yarn to a shank button leaving a 6–8in/15–20cm tail on either side of the knot. Insert button into top of arm and, with a crochet hook, draw both yarn tails out at the same place along the inside of the shoulder. Close hole at the top of the arm. See pg. 91 for example illustration.

FINGERS (make 8)

Rnd 1: With G, 6 sc in adjustable ring—6 sts.

Rnd 2: Sc in each st around. Fasten off. Do not stuff.

Use the handle of the crochet hook to help invert the finger.

Sew fingers to hand. With F, work 3 short sts on back of hand for a glove detail.

CAPE

Row 1: With F, ch 20, sc in 2nd ch from hook and each ch across, turn—19 sts.

Rows 2–5: Ch 1, sc2tog, sc to last 2 sts, sc2tog, turn—11 sts.

Row 6: Ch 1, sc in each st across, turn.

Rows 7–8: Ch 1, 3 sc in next st, sc to last st, 3 sc in last st, turn—19 sts.

Row 9: Ch 1, 2 sc in next st, sc in next 17 sts, 2 sc in next st, turn—21 sts.

Rows 10–30: Ch 1, sc in each st across, turn. Fasten off.

With F, sl st along sides of cape. Press cape with a low heat iron before attaching Row 6 directly under the jacket collar at the back of the body.

JACK THE HEADLESS HORSEMAN

When the moon is full and the fog is heavy, Jack saddles up to go out for a midnight ride with his trusty horse, Nightmare, to stir up some trouble. With his pumpkin head in hand, he would be a truly terrifying sight if only he could keep track of which end of his pumpkin was right-side up.

SKILL LEVEL
—Advanced
Body Height: 5¼in/13.25cm
Head Height:
2¼in/5.75cm, Head Width: 2¾in/7cm

- - - - - - - - - - - - - - - - - - - -

MATERIALS

- Lion Brand Wool Ease® 3oz/85g, 197yds/180m (80% acrylic, 20% wool) —one each: #153 Black (A), #152 Oxford Grey (B), #180 Forest Green Heather (C), #099 Fisherman (D), #129 Cocoa (E), #179 Chestnut Heather (F), #167 Eggplant (G), #171 Gold (H), #199 Pumpkin (J), #174 Avocado (K)

- F-5 (3.75mm) crochet hook

- Black felt [see page 103 for felt templates]

- Fabric glue

- Sewing needle and thread in black

- ½in/1cm plastic shank buttons (2) (optional)

- Earth magnets and 6in/15cm squares of cotton fabric [Small 12–15 mm earth magnet set (2 magnets)] and [Large 18–20 mm earth magnet set (2 magnets*)].

- * One large magnet is used in the horseman, the other in the horse.

BODY

Rnd 1: With B, 10 sc in adjustable ring—10 sts.

Rnd 2: 2 sc in each st around—20 sts.

Rnds 3, 5–6, 9–10: Sc in each st around.

Rnd 4: [Sc in next 3 sts, 2 sc in next st] 5 times—25 sts.

Rnd 7: With C, FPsc in each st around.

Rnd 8: [Sc in next 3 sts, sc2tog] 5 times—20 sts.

Rnd 11: [Sc in next 2 sts, sc2tog] 5 times—15 sts.

Turn body inside out and sew one large earth magnet (page 22) to bottom of body. Turn right side out and stuff body.

Rnd 12: [Sc in next 3 sts, sc2tog] 3 times—12 sts. Pm in 9th st from hook. Fasten off.

Row 13: Join D with (sl st, ch 1, sc) in marked st, sc in next 7 sts, turn—8 sts.

Continue working in only these 8 sts.

Rows 14–15: Ch 1, 2 sc in next st, sc to last st, 2 sc in last st, turn—12 sts.

Row 16: Ch 1, sl st in each st in row. Fasten off. Stuff body.

BELT AND SHIRT EDGE

With E, ch 24 and join with sl st to form a ring.

Rnd 1: Ch 1, 23 sc in ring—23 sts.

Change to dark green.

Rnd 2: With C, BLsl st in each st around.

Rnd 3: BLsc in next 10 sts, (sc, hdc, sc) in BL of next st, BLsl st in next st, pm, (sc, hdc, sc) in BL of next st, BLsc in next 10 sts—27 sts. Fasten off.

With marker in front, slide belt and shirt edge over body to Rnd 6. Remove marker.

With E, sew belt to body leaving shirt edge loose. With H, add a buckle detail with long sts over the front of the belt.

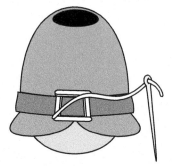

NECK OPENING

Rnd 1: With A, 6 sc in adjustable ring—6 sts.

Rnd 2: 2 sc in each st around—12 sts.

Change to C. Work in the next 6 sts only.

Row 3: With C, sl st in next 6 sts, turn leaving rem sts unworked—6 sts.

Row 4: Ch 1, sl st in next st, (sc, hdc, sc) in next st, sl st in next 2 sts, (sc, hdc, sc) in next st, sl st in next st. Fasten off.

Sew one smaller earth magnet (see page 22) to underside of neck opening piece. Attach to open edge of body with collar points facing front. With A, work a group of satin sts bet collar points, then work a long st on front of body for jacket detail.

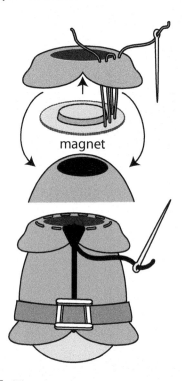

magnet

BOOT AND LEG (make 2)

Rnd 1: With F, 8 sc in adjustable ring—8 sts.

Rnd 2: 2 sc in each st around—16 sts.

Rnds 3, 7: Sc in each st around.

Rnd 4: [Sc in next 7 sts, 2 sc in next st] 2 times—18 sts.

Rnd 5: [Sc in next 7 sts, sc2tog] 2 times—16 sts.

Rnd 6: [Sc in next 2 sts, sc2tog] 4 times—12 sts.

Rnd 8: (ankle opening) Sc in next 4 sts, ch 4, sk 4, sc in next 4 sts.

Rnd 9: Sc in next 4 sts, sc in next 4 ch, sc 4 in next 4 sts. Stuff boot.

Rnd 10: Sc2tog 6 times—6 sts. Fasten off and close hole in back of shoe.

LEG

Rnd 1: Join F in ankle opening at top of boot with (sl st, ch 1, sc) (counts as 1 sc), sc in next 7 sts around inside of ankle opening—8 sts.

Rnds 2–3, 5–6: Sc in each st around.

Rnd 4: With B, [BLsc in next 2 sts, BLsc2tog] 2 times—6 sts.

Rnd 7: [Sc in next 2 sts, 2 sc in next st] 2 times—8 sts. Fasten off. Stuff leg.

BOOT CUFF DETAIL

Rnd 1: With foot pointed down, join F with (sl st, ch 1, sc) in any exposed lp st in Rnd 4, sc in next 7 exposed lps of Rnd 4—8 sts.

Rnd 2: FLsc in each st around.

Rnd 3: Sc in each st around.

Rnd 4: Sl st in each st around. Fasten off.

Fold cuff over ankle of boot and tack in place. Sew open ends of legs to the bottom of horseman's body (avoiding the magnet).

HEEL (make 2)

Row 1: With F, 8 sc in adjustable ring, turn—8 sts.

Row 2: Ch 1, sc in each st across. Fasten off.

With the round edge of heel facing the back of boot, sew in place.

JACKET

Rnd 1: With G, 8 sc in adjustable ring—8 sts.

Rnd 2: [Sc in next st, 3 sc in next st] 4 times—16 sts.

Rnd 3: Sc in next 2 sts, [3 sc in next st, sc in next 3 sts] 3 times, 3 sc in next st, sc in next st—24 sts.

Rnd 4: Sc in next 3 sts, 3 sc in next st, sc in next st, hdc in next 3 sts, sc in next st, 3 sc in next st, (sc, hdc, dc) in next st, (dc, hdc, sl st) in next st, sk 1, (sl st, hdc, dc) in next st, (dc, hdc, sc) in next st, 3 sc in next st, sc in next st, hdc in next 3 sts, sc in next st, 3 sc in next st, sc in next 2 sts—39 sts.

Rnd 5: Sl st in next 4 sts, 3 hdc in next st, hdc in next 2 sts, dc in next 3 sts, hdc in next 2 sts, 3 sc in next st, sc in next 2 sts, hdc in next st, 2 dc in next st, (hdc, sl st) in next st, sl st in next 4 sts, (sl st, hdc) in next st, 2 dc in next st, hdc in next st, sc in next 2 sts, 3 sc in next st, hdc in next 2 sts, dc in next 3 sts, hdc in next 2 sts, 3 hdc in next st, sl st in next 3 sts—51 sts.

Rnd 6: FLsc in next 4 sts, hdc in next st, 3 hdc in next st, hdc in next st, sc in next st, (hdc, dc, hdc) in next st, sk 1, sl st in next 10 sts, (sc, hdc, sc) in next st, sl st in next st, (sc, hdc, sc) in next st, sl st in next 6 sts, (sc, hdc, sc) in next st, sl st in next st, (sc, hdc, sc) in next st, sl st in next 10 sts, sk 1, (hdc, dc, hdc) in next st, sc in next st, hdc in next st, 3 hdc in next st, hdc in next st, FLsc in next 3 sts—65 sts. Count back 4 sts from hook and pm. Fasten off.

COLLAR DETAIL

Row 1: With RS facing, join G with (sl st, ch 1, hdc) in FL of marked st, FLhdc in next 10 sts, turn—11 sts.

Row 2: Ch 1, 2 sc in next st, sc in next 9 sts, 2 sc in next st—13 sts. Fasten off. With RS facing and jacket tails at bottom, wrap top half of jacket around shoulders and sides of body and sew the top and side edges of jacket in place. Leave collar, jacket, jacket's tails, and side edges below the belt loose.

HAND AND ARM (make 2)

Rnd 1: With A, 6 sc in adjustable ring—6 sts.

Rnd 2: 2 sc in each st around—12 sts.

Rnds 3–4, 8–11: Sc in each st around.

Rnd 5: [Sc in next st, sc2tog] 4 times—8 sts.

Rnd 6: Sc in each st around. Stuff hand.

Rnd 7: With G, FPhdc in each st around.

Rnd 12: [Sc in next 2 sts, sc2tog] 2 times—6 sts. Fasten off. Stuff arm, flatten seam and sew closed.

(Optional jointed arms) Tie yarn to a shank button leaving a 6-8in/15–20cm tail on either side of the knot. Insert button into top of arm and, with a crochet hook, draw both yarn tails out at the same place along the inside of the shoulder. Close hole at the top of the arm.

CUFF

Rnd 1: With hand pointed up, join G with (sl st, ch 1, sc) in exposed lp of Rnd 7, sc in next 7 exposed lps of Rnd 7—8 sts.

Rnd 2: FLsc in each st around.

Rnd 3: Sc in each st around.

Rnd 4: Sl st in each st around. Fasten off. Fold cuff over arm and tack down.

Attach arms to jacket at shoulders. If utilizing shank buttons, draw the yarn tails attached to the button through the body and secure the yarn at the opposite shoulder.

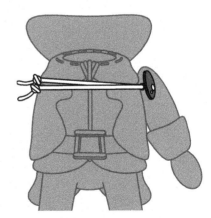

FINGERS (make 8)

Rnd 1: With A, 6 sc in adjustable ring—6 sts.

Rnd 2: Sc in each st around. Fasten off. Do not stuff. Sew open edges of fingers to hand.

PUMPKIN HEAD

Rnd 1: With J, 6 sc in adjustable ring—6 sts.

Rnd 2: 2 sc in each st around—12 sts.

Rnd 3: [Sc in next st, 2 sc in next st] 6 times—18 sts.

Rnd 4: [Sc in next 2 sts, 2 sc in next st] 6 times—24 sts.

Rnd 5: [Sc in next 3 sts, 2 sc in next st] 6 times—30 sts.

Rnds 6–9: Sc in each sc around.

Rnd 10: [Sc in next 4 sts, 2 sc in next st] 6 times—36 sts.

Rnds 11–12: Sc in each st around.

Sew the 2nd small magnet to interior floor of pumpkin (check to make sure it's facing the right way to connect with the horseman's neck before securing).

Rnd 13: [Sc in next 4 sts, sc2tog] 6 times—30 sts.

Rnds 14–17: Sc in each st around.

Rnd 18: [Sc in next 3 sts, sc2tog] 6 times—24 sts.

Rnd 19: [Sc in next 2 sts, sc2tog] 6 times—18 sts.

Rnd 20: [Sc in next st, sc2tog] 6 times—12 sts. Stuff.

Rnd 21: Sc2tog 6 times—6 sts. Fasten off yarn.

With E, work long sts from the middle top of pumpkin to the bottom (avoiding the magnet area) 7 times, pulling firmly to shape pumpkin ridges.

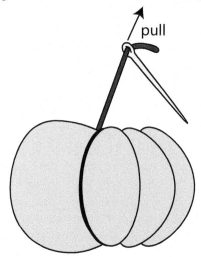

PUMPKIN LEAF AND VINE (make 3)

With K, ch 6–9 sts. Sl st in 3rd ch from hook, ch 3, sl st in base of ch-3, ch 3, sl st in base of ch- 3, sl st in next st of ch-6 (7, 8, 9) and fasten off. Weave yarn tail through to the end of the ch.

Attach leaves to the top of the pumpkin.

PUMPKIN STEM

Rnd 1: With E, 6 sc in adjustable ring—6 sts.

Rnd 2: BLsc in each st around.

Rnds 3–4: Sc in each st around. Fasten off. Attach stem to top of pumpkin.

FINISHING

Cut pumpkin eyes (either angry or confused) from black felt and sew or glue to pumpkin. With A, embroider a mouth and eyebrows onto pumpkin face.

NIGHTMARE
THE HORSE

The ghostly clicks of horse hooves in the darkness can only mean that terror is approaching in the form of Nightmare, the devil horse of Jack, the Headless Horseman! With glowing red eyes and a midnight-blue mane, this mare of the night is a sight that's sure to scare the wits out of any poor soul who gets in her way.

SKILL LEVEL
—Advanced
Height: 8½in/21.5cm, including ears

- - - - - - - - - - - - - - - - - - - -

MATERIALS

- Lion Brand Wool Ease® 3oz/85g, 197yds/180m (80% acrylic, 20% wool) —one each: #153 Black (A), #129 Cocoa (B), #114 Denim (C)
- Lion Brand® Pelt 1.75oz/50g, 47yds/43m (68% Nylon, 32% Polyester)— one each: #201 Blue Mink (D)
- F-5 (3.75mm) crochet hook
- Red (poinsettia) felt and black felt [see page 103 for felt templates]
- Earth magnet set (optional)
- Black pipe cleaners (4)
- Fabric glue
- Sewing needle and thread in red and black

HORSE BODY

Rnd 1: With A, 8 sc in adjustable ring—8 sts.

Rnd 2: [Sc in next st, 2 sc in next st] 4 times—12 sts.

Rnd 3: [Sc in next 2 sts, 2 sc in next st] 4 times—16 sts.

Rnd 4: [Sc in next 3 sts, 2 sc in next st] 4 times—20 sts.

Rnd 5: [Sc in next 4 sts, 2 sc in next st] 4 times—24 sts.

Rnd 6: [Sc in next 5 sts, 2 sc in next st] 4 times—28 sts.

Rnd 7: (neck opening) Sc in next 2 sts, ch 9, sk 9, sc in next 17 sts—28 sts.

Rnd 8: Sc in next 2 sts, sc in next 9 ch, sc in next 17 sts—28 sts.

Rnds 9–16, 18, 21: Sc in each st around.

Rnd 17: [Sc in next 5 sts, sc2tog] 4 times—24 sts.

Rnd 19: [Sc in next 5 sts, 2 sc in next st] 4 times—28 sts.

Rnd 20: [Sc in next 6 sts, 2 sc in next st] 4 times—32 sts.

Rnd 22: [Sc in next 2 sts, sc2tog] 8 times—24 sts.

Rnd 23: [Sc in next 2 sts, sc2tog] 6 times—18 sts. Stuff body.

Rnd 24: [Sc in next st, sc2tog] 6 times—12 sts.

Rnd 25: Sc2tog 6 times—6 sts. Fasten off.

NECK

Rnd 1: Join A in lower corner of neck opening with (sl st, ch 1, sc) in same st (counts as 1 sc), sc in next 17 sts around inside of neck opening—18 sts.

Rnds 2–5: Sc in each st around. Fasten off. Stuff neck.

FRONT LEG (make 2)

Rnd 1: With C, 6 sc in adjustable ring—6 sts.

Rnd 2: 2 sc in next st, 2 hdc in next 4 sts, 2 sc in next st—12 sts.

Rnd 3: BLsl st in next 2 sts, BLsc in next 2 sts, BLhdc in next 4 sts, BLsc in next 2 sts, BLsl st in next 2 sts—12 sts.

Rnd 4: Sc in next 4 sts, hdc in next 4 sts, sc in next 4 sts.

Rnd 5: Sc2tog, sc in next 8 sts, sc2tog—10 sts.

Rnd 6: Sc2tog, sc in next 6 sts, sc2tog—8 sts. Stuff hoof.

Rnd 7: With A, Fpsc in each st around.

Rnd 8: [Sc in next st, 2 sc in next st] 4 times—12 sts. Stuff lower leg.

Rnd 9: [Sc in next st, sc2tog] 4 times—8 sts.

Rnds 10–13, 15, 17: Sc in each st around.

Rnd 14: [Sc in next st, 2 sc in next st] 4 times—12 sts.

Rnd 16: [Sc in next st, sc2tog] 4 times—8 sts.

Rnd 18: [Sc in next 3 sts, 2 sc in next st] 2 times—10 sts.

Rnd 19: [Sc in next 4 sts, 2 sc in next st] 2 times—12 sts.

LEFT FRONT LEG SHOULDER ONLY

Row 20: 2 sc in next 5 sts, turn leaving rem sts unworked—10 sts.

Row 21: Ch 1, 2 sc in next st, sc in next 2 sts, hdc in next 4 sts, sc in next 2 sts, 2 sc in next st, turn—12 sts.

Row 22: Ch 1, sc in next 4 sts, hdc in next 4 sts, sc in next 4 sts. Fasten off.

RIGHT FRONT LEG SHOULDER ONLY

Row 20: Turn, ch 1, sl st in next 2 sts, 2 sc in next 5 sts, turn leaving rem sts unworked—10 sc.

Row 21: Ch 1, 2 sc in next st, sc in next 2 sts, hdc in next 4 sts, sc in next 2 sts, 2 sc in next st, turn—12 sts.

Row 22: Ch 1, sc in next 4 sts, hdc in next 4 sts, sc in next 4 sts. Fasten off.

BACK LEG (make 2)

Rnd 1: With C, 6 sc in adjustable ring—6 sts.

Rnd 2: 2 sc in next st, 2 hdc in next 4 sts, 2 sc in next st—12 sts.

Rnd 3: BLsl st in next 2 sts, BLsc in next 2 sts, BLhdc in next 4 sts, BLsc in next 2 sts, BLsl st in next 2 sts.

Rnd 4: Sc in next 4 sts, hdc in next 4 sts, sc in next 4 sts.

Rnd 5: Sc2tog, sc in next 8 sts, sc2tog—10 sts.

Rnd 6: Sc2tog, sc in next 6 sts, sc2tog—8 sts. Stuff hoof.

Rnd 7: With A, FPsc in each st around.

Rnd 8: [Sc in next st, 2 sc in next st] 4 times—12 sts.

Rnd 9: [Sc in next st, sc2tog] 4 times—8 sts.

Rnds 10–13: Sc in each st around.

Rnd 14: [Sc in next st, 2 sc in next st] 4 times—12 sts. Stuff lower leg.

Rnd 15: (upper leg opening) Sc in next 7 sts, ch 4, sk 1 (pm in skipped st), sk 3, sc in next st—12 sts.

Rnd 16: Sc2tog 3 times, sc in next st, sc in next 4 ch—8 sts. Fasten off.

Rnd 17: Join A in upper leg opening with (sl st, ch 1, sc) in marked st (counts as 1 sc), sc in next 7 sts around upper leg opening—8 sts.

Rnd 18: [Sc in next 3 sts, 2 sc in next st] 2 times—10 sts.

Rnd 19: [Sc in next 4 sts, 2 sc in next st] 2 times—12 sts.

Rnd 20: [Sc in next 5 sts, 2 sc in next st] 2 times—14 sts.

LEFT BACK LEG HIP ONLY

Row 21: Sc in next 4 sts, 2 sc in next 2 sts, turn leaving rem sts unworked—8 sts.

Row 22: Ch 1, 2 sc in next st, sc in next 4 sts, hdc in next 4 sts, sc in next 2 sts, 2 sc in next st, turn—14 sts.

Row 23: Ch 1, sc in next 2 sts, hdc in next 4 sts, sc in next 4 sts, sl st in next 2 sts, turn—12 sts.

Row 24: Ch 1, sk 1, sc in next st, hdc in next 6 sts, sc in next st, sk 1, sl st in next st, turn—9 sts.

Row 25: Ch 1, sk 1, sl st in next st, sc in next 6 sts. Fasten off.

RIGHT BACK LEG HIP ONLY

Row 21: Ch 1, turn work, sl st in next 3 sts, sc in next 4 sts, 2 sc in next 2 sts, turn leaving rem sts unworked—8 sc.

Row 22: Ch 1, 2 sc in next st, sc in next 4 sts, hdc in next 4 sts, sc in next 2 sts, 2sc in next st, turn—14 sts.

Row 23: Ch 1, sc in next 2 sts, hdc in next 4 sts, sc in next 4 sts, sl st in next 2 sts, turn—12 sts.

Row 24: Ch 1, sk 1, sc in next st, hdc in next 6 sts, sc in next st, sk 1, sl st in next st, turn— 9 sts.

Row 25: Ch 1, sk 1, sl st in next st, sc in next 6 sts. Fasten off.

Close holes in backs of knees. Finish stuffing legs firmly, reinforcing with pipe cleaners, if necessary.

Following pipe cleaner technique (see pages 22–23), add pipe cleaners to legs if desired for extra posability and stability. If stuffing in lower leg shifts while installing pipe cleaners, redistribute it by grabbing and moving bits around with a crochet hook through surface of leg.

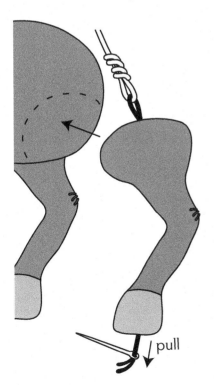

HEAD

Rnd 1: With A, 8 sc in adjustable ring—8 sts.

Rnd 2: [Sc in next st, 2 sc in next st] 4 times—12 sts.

Rnd 3: [Sc in next 3 sts, 2 sc in next st] 3 times—15 sts.

Rnds 4, 6, 9–12, 14: Sc in each st around.

Rnd 5: [Sc in next 3 sts, sc2tog] 3 times—12 sts.

Rnd 7: [Sc in next 2 sts, 2 sc in next st] 4 times—16 sts.

Rnd 8: [Sc in next st, 2 sc in next st] 8 times—24 sts.

Rnd 13: [Sc in next 5 sts, 2 sc in next st] 4 times—28 sts.

Rnd 15: [Sc in next 5 sts, sc2tog] 4 times— 24 sts.

Rnd 16: [Sc in next st, sc2tog] 8 times—16 sts. Stuff head.

Rnd 17: Sc2tog 8 times—8 sts. Fasten off and close hole in back of head. Sew head to open edge of neck.

MOUTH

Row 1: With A, 8 sc in adjustable ring, turn—8 sts.

Row 2: Ch 1, sc in each st across. Fasten off. Sew straight edge of jaw 7 rnds back from front of head.

NOSTRIL (make 2)

With A, 5 sc in adjustable ring. Fasten off. Do not pull ring completely closed, space in center will serve as nostril opening. Sew nostrils to front of muzzle on either side of Rnd 1 with the adjustable ring facing up.

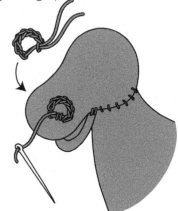

EARS (make 2)

Rnd 1: With A, ch 4, sc in 2nd ch from hook and in next ch, 5 hdc in next ch. Rotate ch so front loops are facing up. Sc in next ch, 2 FLsc in next ch—10 sts.

Rnd 2: Ch 2, sl st in next 2 sts, sc in next 5 sts, sl st in next 3 sts.

Rnd 3: (Sc, sl st) in ch-2 sp. Fasten off. Using tail from beg of work, pinch bottom of ear tog and tack in place. Sew ears to top of head spaced about 3 sts apart.

EYEBROW (make 2)

Rnd 1: With A, ch 7, sl st in 2nd ch from hook, sc in next st, hdc in next 2 ch, sc in next ch, sl st in next ch. Fasten off.

Cut two eyes from red felt and two pupils from black felt. Glue or sew eyes to the sides of the horse's head.

Sew eyelids around back and top edge of eyes.

BRIDLE

With B, ch 20. Fasten off. Tie ch around muzzle of horse and secure under chin.

Ch 27. Fasten off. Tie ch around head (just in front of ears) and secure where chin meets neck.

Ch 30. Fasten off. Laying center of ch behind ears. Work each end under bridle straps on each side of face. Tie ends together in horse's mouth and secure with a couple of sts. Secure the points where bridle pieces cross by wrapping yarn in an "X" pattern around them. Draw the yarn through the head and secure points

where straps cross on the other side of head before securing ends and weaving in tails.

Ch 40. Fasten off. Attach end of ch to bridle at corners of mouth.

SADDLE PART 1

Rnd 1: With B, ch 6, sc in 2nd ch from hook and in next 3 ch, 5 sc in next ch. Rotate ch so front loops are facing up. Sc in next 3 ch, 4 sc in next ch—16 sts.

Rnd 2: [3 sc in next st, sc in next 3 sts] 4 times—24 sts.

Rnd 3: Sc in next st, [3 sc in next st, sc in next 5 sts] 3 times, 3 sc in next st, sc in next 4 sts—32 sts.

Rnd 4: [Ch 12, hdc in 2nd ch from hook and next 10 ch, sl st at base of ch, sl st in next 15 sts] 2 times, sl st in next 2 sts. Fasten off.

SADDLE PART 2

Rnd 1: With B, ch 9, sc in 2nd ch from hook and next 6 ch, 5 sc in next ch. Rotate ch so front loops are facing up. Sc in next 6 ch, 4 sc in next ch—22 sts.

Rnd 2: [3 sc in next st, sc in next 6 sts, 3 sc in next st, sc in next 3 sts] 2 times—30 sts.

Rnd 3: Sc in next st, *3 sc in next st, sc in next 8 sts, 3 sc in next st**, sc in next 5 sts, rep from *to**, sc in next 4 sts—38 sts.

FINISHING

Sew legs to body, stuffing upper portions before closing seams. With D, work 5–6 lines of backstitches along the back of neck and between ears for the mane. Use a comb or tapestry needle to gently loosen up fur. With C, cinch the hooves at the top of back through the bottom center. With D, backstitch around top of hoof and trim fur to ¼–½in/.5–1cm.

Place RS of saddle part 2 against WS of saddle part 1 in a cross shape and sew tog. Add an earth magnet bet pieces, if desired. Check to make sure magnet is oriented correctly to stick to magnet in body of horseman. Sew straps on saddle part 1 underneath horse's belly. Tack saddle in place.

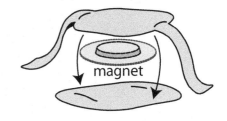

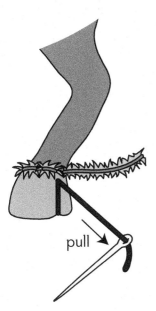

With D, holding hand flat, wrap yarn loosely around 4 fingers 5 times. Tie tails around looped strands and attach to back of horse for tail. Trim to desired length.

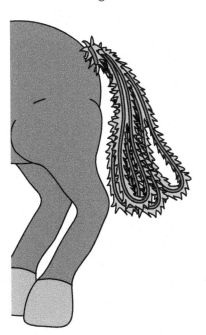

BOO BOO THE VOODOO DOLL

Boo Boo the Voodoo Doll loves nothing more than getting hugs, kisses, and a well-placed pin or two if any of your friends get out of line. Make a little Boo Boo Voodoo Doll for all the special people in your life!

SKILL LEVEL
—Beginner

Height while sitting: 6in/15.25cm, including hair

- - - - - - - - - - - - - - - - - - -

MATERIALS

- Cascade 220® 3½oz/100g, 220yds/200m (100% Peruvian Highland Wool)—one each: #0980 Pesto (A), #8622 Camel (B), #8555 Black (C)
- F-5 (3.75mm) crochet hook
- ¾–1in/2–2.5cm 4-hole wooden button
- Fiberfill stuffing
- Scissors
- Tapestry needle

BODY AND HEAD

Rnd 1: With A, 10 sc in adjustable ring—10 sts.

Rnd 2: 2 sc in each st around—20 sts.

Rnd 3: [Sc in next st, 2 sc in next st] 10 times—30 sts.

Rnds 4–7, 9–10: Sc in each st around.

Rnd 8: [Sc in next st, sc2tog] 10 times—20 sts.

Rnd 11: [Sc in next 3 sts, sc2tog] 4 times—16 sts.

Rnd 12: [Sc in next 2 sts, sc2tog] 4 times—12 sts.

Rnd 13: [Sc in next st, sc2tog] 4 times—8 sts. Stuff body firmly.

Rnd 14: (neck) 2 FLsc in each st around—16 sts.

Rnd 15: [Sc in next st, 2 sc in next st] 8 times—24 sts.

Rnd 16: [Sc in next 2 sts, 2 sc in next st] 8 times—32 sts.

Rnd 17: [Sc in next 3 sts, 2 sc in next st] 8 times—40 sts.

Rnds 18, 20, 22: Sc in each st around.

Rnd 19: [Sc in next 4 sts, 2 sc in next st] 8 times—48 sts.

Rnd 21: [Sc in next 4 sts, sc2tog] 8 times—40 sts.

Rnd 23: [Sc in next 3 sts, sc2tog] 8 times—32 sts.

Rnd 24: [Sc in next 2 sts, sc2tog] 8 times—24 sts.

Rnd 25: [Sc in next st, sc2tog] 8 times—16 sts. Stuff head firmly.

Rnd 26: Sc2tog 8 times—8 sc. Fasten off, finish stuffing, close hole, and weave in ends.

ARMS AND LEGS

Rnd 1: With A, ch 4, 2 sc in 2nd ch from hook, 5 sc in next ch. Rotate ch so front loops are facing up. Sc in next ch, 4 sc in next ch—12 sts.

Rnd 2: [Sc in next 2 sts, 2 sc in next st] 4 times—16 sts.

Rnds 3, 6–7: Sc in each st around.

Rnd 4: [Sc in next 2 sts, sc2tog] 4 times—12 sts.

Rnd 5: [Sc in next 4 sts, sc2tog] 2 times—10 sts.

Rnd 8: [Sc in next 3 sts, sc2tog] 2 times—8 sts. Stuff limb.

Rnd 9: [Sc in next 2 sts, sc2tog] 2 times—6 sts. Fasten off. Flatten seam and whip stitch closed.

FINISHING

Sew arms and legs to the shoulders and hips of the body. Weave in ends. With B, backstitch a vertical line down center of each arm (from shoulder to underarm), each leg (from hips to under-leg), body, and head. Work short sts across each line as illustrated.

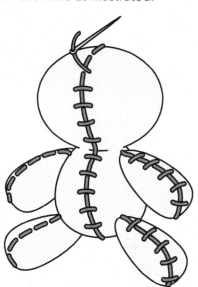

With C, make a long st across the face for a smile. Shape with marking pins. Work small X's over the line.

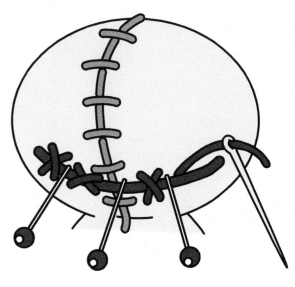

With C, work an X to secure one wooden button for an eye. Sew an X for the second eye. Embroider eyebrows. Cut 7 10in/25.5cm pieces of A and make a tightly grouped fringe on the top of the head (see page 21). Wrap a length of B 7–8 times around the fringe 1in/2.5cm above the top of the head and secure. Trim fringe to desired length.

FELT TEMPLATES

Note: Trace these templates for use with patterns.

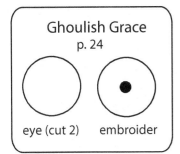

Ghoulish Grace
p. 24

eye (cut 2)   embroider

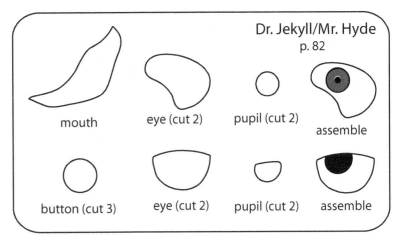

Dr. Jekyll/Mr. Hyde
p. 82

mouth   eye (cut 2)   pupil (cut 2)   assemble

button (cut 3)   eye (cut 2)   pupil (cut 2)   assemble

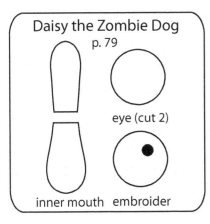

Daisy the Zombie Dog
p. 79

eye (cut 2)

inner mouth   embroider

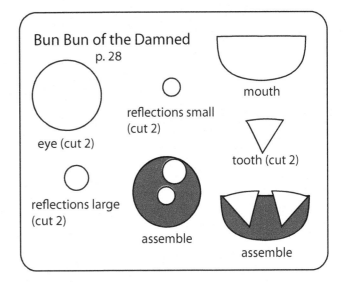

Bun Bun of the Damned
p. 28

eye (cut 2)

reflections small
(cut 2)

reflections large
(cut 2)

mouth

tooth (cut 2)

assemble   assemble

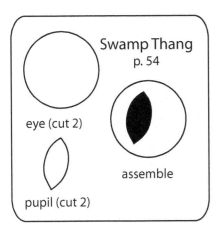

Swamp Thang
p. 54

eye (cut 2)

assemble

pupil (cut 2)

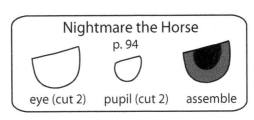

Nightmare the Horse
p. 94

eye (cut 2)   pupil (cut 2)   assemble

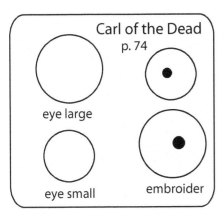

Carl of the Dead
p. 74

eye large

eye small   embroider

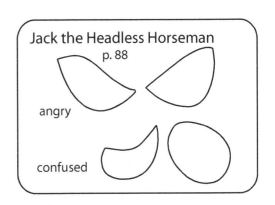

Jack the Headless Horseman
p. 88

angry

confused

FELT TEMPLATES

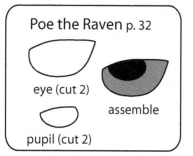

Poe the Raven p. 32

eye (cut 2)

assemble

pupil (cut 2)

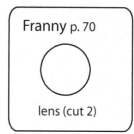

Franny p. 70

lens (cut 2)

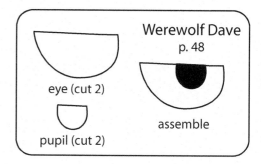

Werewolf Dave p. 48

eye (cut 2)

assemble

pupil (cut 2)

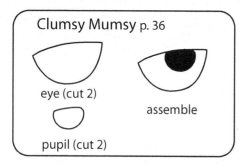

Clumsy Mumsy p. 36

eye (cut 2)

assemble

pupil (cut 2)

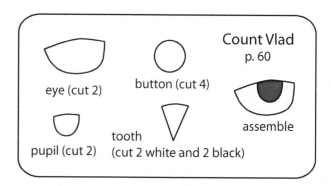

Count Vlad p. 60

eye (cut 2)

button (cut 4)

pupil (cut 2)

tooth
(cut 2 white and 2 black)

assemble

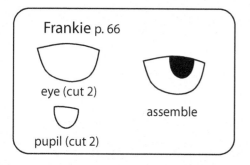

Frankie p. 66

eye (cut 2)

assemble

pupil (cut 2)

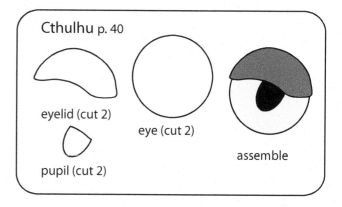

Cthulhu p. 40

eyelid (cut 2)

eye (cut 2)

pupil (cut 2)

assemble

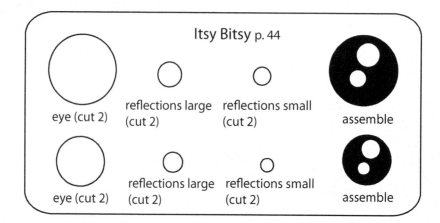

Itsy Bitsy p. 44

eye (cut 2)

reflections large
(cut 2)

reflections small
(cut 2)

assemble

eye (cut 2)

reflections large
(cut 2)

reflections small
(cut 2)

assemble

ABBREVIATIONS

( )	Work instructions within parentheses as many times as directed.
*	Repeat instructions following the single asterisk as directed.
alt	alternate
approx	approximately
beg	begin(ning)
bet	between
BL	back loop only
BLhdc	back loop half double crochet
BLsc	back loop single crochet
BPdc	back post double crochet
BPsc	back post single crochet
ch	chain / chain stitch
ch sp	chain space
cont	continue(ing)
dc	double crochet
FL	front loop only
FLsc	front loop single crochet
FPdc	front post double crochet
FPhdc	front post half double crochet
FPsc	front post single crochet
g	gram(s)
hdc	half double crochet
in	inch(es)
lp(s)	loop(s)
m	meter(s)
mm	millimeter(s)
oz	ounce(s)
pm	place marker
prev	previous
rem	remaining
rep	repeat(s)
rnd(s)	round(s)
RS	right side
sc	single crochet
sc2tog	single crochet 2 together
sk	skip
sl	slip
sl st	slip stitch
sp	space
st(s)	stitch(es)
tog	together
tr	triple crochet
tbl	through both loops
WS	wrong side
yd(s)	yard(s)
YO	yarn over

YARN WEIGHTS

1	super fine
2	fine
3	light
4	medium
5	bulky
6	super bulky

CROCHET HOOK SIZES & CONVERSIONS

METRIC SIZES(mm)	US SIZES	UK/CAN
2.0	-	14
2.25	B/1	13
2.5	-	12
2.75	C/2	-
3.0	-	11
3.25	D/3	10
3.5	E/4	9
3.75	F/5	-
4.0	G/6	8
4.5	7	7
5.0	H/8	6
5.5	I/9	5
6.0	J/10	4
6.5	K/10 1/2	3
7.0	-	2
8.0	L/11	0
9.0	M/13	00
10.0	N/15	000

PATTERN YARNS

BOO BOO THE VOODOO DOLL
Cascade 220®: Pesto (0980), Camel (8622), Black (8555)

BUN BUN OF THE DAMNED
Lion Brand® Wool Ease®: Black (153), Blush Heather (104), White Frost (501)
Felt: White, Red (poinsettia)

CARL OF THE DEAD
Knit Picks® Wool of the Andes: Pampas Heather (24074), Cadet (25070), Blossom Heather (25067), Brown Sugar (25985), Victorian (25980), Coal (23420), Cloud (23432)
Felt: Yellow (sunshine)

CLUMSY MUMSY
Red Heart® Soft®: Toast (1882), Black (4614)
Red Heart® Boutique™ Sashay®: Aran (1112)
Felt: Black, Yellow (buttercream)

COUNT VLAD
Cascade 220®: Black (8555), White (8505), Natural (8010), Ruby (9404), Sunflower (2415)
Felt: White, Black, Dark red (beet), Light yellow (sunshine)

CTHULHU
Berroco Vintage®: Gingham (5120), Minty (5112)
Felt: Black, Light green (honeydew), Medium green (cabbage)

DAISY THE ZOMBIE DOG
Knit Picks® Wool of the Andes: Opal Heather (25645), Brown Sugar (25985), Coal (23420), Victorian (25980), Cloud (23432)
Felt: Yellow (sunshine), Black

DR. JEKYLL AND MR. HYDE
Knit Picks® Wool of the Andes: Oyster Heather (24649), Coal (23420), Fedora (24277), Cloud (23432), Marble Heather (25976), Bittersweet Heather (24652), Garnet Heather (25633)
Felt: Red (big apple), Gray (stone), Black, White, Light yellow (buttercream)

FRANKIE
Cascade 220®: Primavera (8903), Lily Pad (9637), Smoke (8408), White (8505), Black (8555), Van Dyke Brown (7822), Grey (8509)
Felt: Black, Light yellow (buttercream)

FRANNY
Cascade 220®: Frosty Green (9636), Sand (9499), Natural (8010), Dusk (9614), White (8505), Black (8555), Grey (8509), Van Dyke Brown (7822)
Felt: White

GHOULISH GRACE
Red Heart® Soft®: Black (4614), White (4600), Mid Blue (9820)
Felt: White, Light green (honeydew)

ITSY BITSY
Berroco Vintage®: Black Currant (5182), Oats (5105), Cast Iron (5145), Juniper (5188)
Felt: Black, White

JACK THE HEADLESS HORSEMAN
Lion Brand® Wool Ease®: Black (153), Oxford Grey (152), Forest Green Heather (180), Fisherman (099), Eggplant (167), Cocoa (129), Chestnut Heather (179), Gold (171), Pumpkin (199), Avocado (174)
Felt: Black

NIGHTMARE THE HORSE
Lion Brand® Wool Ease®: Black (153), Denim (114), Cocoa (129)
Lion Brand® Pelt: Blue Mink (201)
Felt: Red (poinsettia), Black

POE THE RAVEN
Red Heart® Soft®: Black (4614), Charcoal (9010)
Felt: Black, Gray (storm cloud)

SWAMP THANG
Berroco Vintage®: Buttercream (5102), Cast Iron (5145), Watermelon (5126), Aster (5114), Kiwi (5124), Clary (51103) Felt: Black, Light yellow (buttercream)

WEREWOLF DAVE
Lion Brand® Wool Ease®: Natural Heather (098), Denim (114), Cocoa (129), Mushroom (403), Black (153)
Lion Brand Pelt: Sable (321-205)
Felt: Black, Light yellow (buttercream)

RESOURCES

Berroco
www.berroco.com
Berroco Yarn

Coats and Clark
www.coatsandclark.com
Red Heart Yarn

Lion Brand
www.lionbrandyarn.com
Lion Brand Yarn

Cascade
http://www.cascadeyarns.com/
Cascade Yarn

Knit Picks
www.knitpicks.com
Online retailer of fine yarns and notions

Hobbs Bonded Fibers
www.hobbsbondedfibers.com
Poly-down fiberfill toy stuffing and black
batting, available at local craft stores

Clover
www.clover-usa.com
Hooks and notions, available at local craft
stores

Fiskars
www.fiskars.com
Scissors and cutting mats, available at local
craft stores

American Felt and Craft
www.americanfeltandcraft.com
Online retailer of fine wool felts and toy
noisemaker inserts

Ingute's Shop
http://www.etsy.com/shop/INGUTE
Handmade wooden buttons

ACKNOWLEDGMENTS

Thank you to Vanessa Putt and the fine folks at Dover Publications who asked me to work on this terrifyingly fun collection of patterns. It's been a scream!

Thank you to all my yarn donors at Knit Picks, Berroco, Red Heart, Lion Brand, and Cascade for being so speedy and generous with their materials and to Andie Clark from American Felt and Craft for spoiling me with a huge stack of beautiful craft felt.

Thank you to Erin Buterbaugh for your support and guidance through the truly horrifying process of contract negotiations.

And, finally, thank you to my husband, Michael, and my children, James and Emily, for putting up with the yarn monster that resides in your home.

ABOUT THE AUTHOR

Megan Kreiner grew up on Long Island, New York, in a household where art and art projects were a daily part of life. Coming from a long line of knitters and crocheters, Megan learned the craft at an early age from her grandmother, her aunt, and her mother. As of 2012, her MK Crochet pattern line has been published and featured in books and various crochet and knitting magazines.

A graduate with a fine arts degree in computer graphics and animation from the University of Massachusetts, Amherst, Megan is pursuing a career in the feature animation industry in Los Angeles and currently works as an animator at DreamWorks Animation.

Megan lives in Altadena, California, with her husband, Michael, and their children, James and Emily. View her work at www.MKCrochet.com.

mk crochet®

Make Your Own
DECORATIVE BOXES
with Easy-to-Use Patterns

Karen Kjældgård-Larsen

DOVER PUBLICATIONS, INC.
New York

Bibliographical Note

Make Your Own Decorative Boxes with Easy-to-Use Patterns, first published by Dover Publications, Inc., in 1995, is a new English-language adaptation of the volume *Smukke æsker efter Kamma Rahbek princippet*, originally published by Forlaget Olivia, Copenhagen, in 1990. The present edition is published by special arrangement with the Danish publisher and the author, c/o Evelyne Johnson Associates, 201 East 28 Street, New York, N.Y. 10016.

Library of Congress Cataloging-in-Publication Data

Kjældgård-Larsen, Karen, 1974–
    Make your own decorative boxes with easy-to-use patterns / Karen Kjældgård-Larsen.
        p.   cm.
    "English-language adaptation of the volume, Smukke æsker efter Kamma Rahbek princippet, originally published by Forlaget Olivia, Copenhagen, in 1990"—T.p. verso.
    ISBN 0-486-27814-X (pbk.)
    1. Box making.   2. Ornamental boxes.   I. Kjældgård-Larsen, Karen, 1974–   Smukke æsker efter Kamma Rahbek princippet. English.   II. Title.
TT970.5.K43   1995
745.593—dc20   94-44866
                                                                                CIP

Manufactured in the United States of America
Dover Publications, Inc., 31 East 2nd Street, Mineola, N.Y. 11501

Materials and Tools

As with any other handcraft, it is naturally important to have the right materials to work with.

Cardboard, pasteboard or a similar heavy paper is the foundation of the boxes. Various weights of paper can be used, and you can experiment with the cardboard you happen to have around. For most boxes, however, the best would be 9-point uncoated board. The cardboard can be purchased at paper and art-supply shops.

The boxes are covered with a different type of paper. Nowadays a very large selection of decorative papers is available. Paper that is used chiefly for wrapping gifts can be purchased in rolls, in loose sheets and in portfolios. But not all giftwrap paper is equally suitable for boxes. It is hard to give general guidelines, but the paper must be neither too thin nor too shiny. This applies especially to boxes with rounded shapes. In these cases the glue or tape will sometimes be visible through the paper if it is too thin.

Naturally you can easily achieve a flashy result with smooth, shiny paper but it is substantially easier to work with matt paper.

Besides "everyday" giftwrap paper, there is a wide assortment of papers by the famous English painter William Morris, as well as a number of Italian-inspired papers. These papers are sometimes expensive, but they are extremely well suited to box making.*

As extra internal decoration you can use glossy pictures, photos or the like, which can be pasted into the lid or bottom of the box. You can also decorate it with "lace" cut out of cake doilies of paper or foil.

To enlarge the patterns you will need graph paper and possibly carbon paper or waxed paper.

The tools you need to make the boxes are: scissors, straightedge (ruler), a craft knife with a sharp blade (such as an X-ACTO), glue (for example, a glue stick) and tape.

---

*[Dover publishes an extensive line of inexpensive giftwrap papers, including the types mentioned here.]

Procedure*

The patterns in this book are to be enlarged with the aid of graph paper (except for those patterns which are reproduced full size).

Be very accurate when measuring. Multiply the measurements in the book up to the size you desire and draw them over on graph paper.

Using a piece of carbon paper, transfer the outlines of the pattern onto the pieces of cardboard and giftwrap you have chosen. You can also cut out the graph-paper enlargement and paste it onto the piece of cardboard that is later to be cut out.

Before you cut into the pattern and the cardboard, you should first decide whether you want to cut outside the lines, inside the lines or right on the lines. This is important because even small irregularities will be visible in the finished product, so be consistent in your cutting.

It pays to be precise and careful with the measuring, the cutting and the assembly.

The procedure for the individual boxes will be clear from the photos in the book.

*[Rita Weiss's book *The Artist's and Craftsman's Guide to Reducing, Enlarging and Transferring Designs* (Dover 0-486-24142-4) contains details on the procedures briefly mentioned here, and includes various types of translucent graph paper.]

Making Angled Boxes

1. This series of photos and instructions covers the construction of angled boxes, whether Florentine, square, oblong, long, triangular or pentagonal, and refers to the patterns on pages 9–20. After drawing all the patterns to their proper size and cutting them out, the measurements indicated on the pattern numbered 7 in each set (except the Florentine box) should be marked off on the piece of cardboard corresponding to that pattern. Thus, if you are making an oblong box and using the patterns on pages 13 and 14 at the size indicated there, these measurements will be 8.4, 5.9, 8.4 and 5.9 centimeters (roughly speaking, 2.5 cm = 1 inch). You should not yet cut away the narrow stub on the end. (The photos here specifically show this oblong box.)

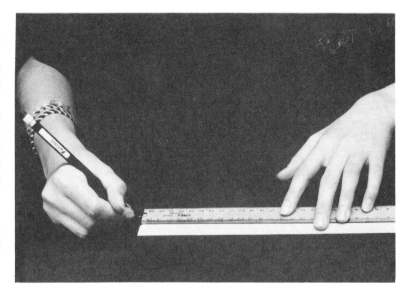

2. Lay a straightedge along the lines that have been marked off (the lines corresponding to the dashed lines on the pattern piece), and press down on them with either an X-ACTO (or similar knife) or the point of a scissors blade. This should be done gently, since the intention is not to cut all the way through the paper. (This procedure, which makes folding easier and neater, is called scoring.)

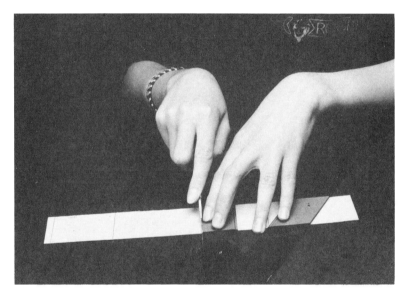

3. Next take the cardboard pieces corresponding to pattern pieces 1 and 2 and score lightly from corner to corner all the way around (on the lines corresponding to the dashed lines on the patterns).

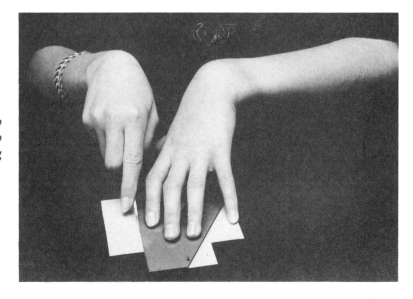

4.   Place cardboard piece 1 in front of you and glue giftwrap piece 4 (the piece of giftwrap paper corresponding to pattern 4) onto the cardboard as shown. Fold the sides of the cardboard upward and put tape on the edges (see also photo 6).

5.   Place cardboard piece 2 in front of you and glue giftwrap piece 3 onto the bottom and up the sides. (This does not mean that the giftwrap paper should reach all the way up to the edge of the cardboard.) It is a good idea to glue only at the sides; this prevents the giftwrap from creasing on the bottom.

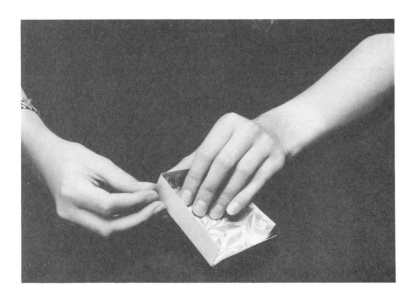

6.   Fold the sides upward and put tape on the edges. This should be done very accurately and closely, or else the box is liable to turn out crooked.

7.   Now use giftwrap pieces 5 and 6. Piece 6 is used for the lid (with the narrower flaps), and Piece 5 for the box bottom (with the wider flaps). Place the cardboard lid and box bottom on the appropriate pieces of gift-wrap and apply glue thoroughly on the sides with the tabs. (The photo shows a glue stick being used.)

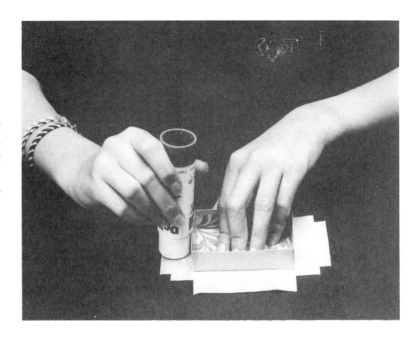

8.   Fold the short sides upward. The small tabs are bent around the sides, and the last tab is bent in, inside the lid or box. Put glue on the long sides and fold them upward around the sides of the cardboard piece and into the lid or box.

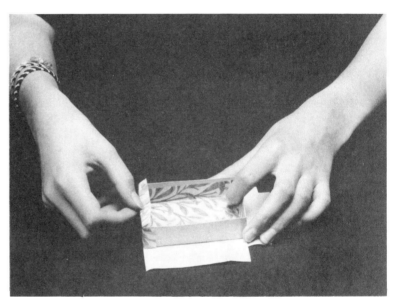

9.   Cardboard piece 7 is now placed inside the box. Check to see if it fits. If it is slightly too loose or too tight or just can't be pressed down in the box, you must adapt it in the best way possible. If you have been careful when cutting out pieces, there should be no problem. If the insert fits the way it should, now cut off the narrow stub on the end.

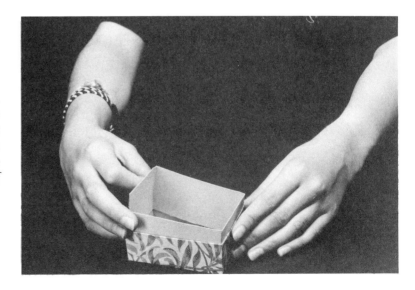

10. Place giftwrap piece 8 flat on the table. Apply glue to the inside of cardboard piece 7 and place it, glue side down, on the giftwrap, about 2 cm from one long edge, and 1 cm from the other. The giftwrap should be slightly longer than the cardboard.

11. Turn the piece over and run the straight edge over it firmly to press out any creases—even those the eye can barely see.

12. Cut one end of the giftwrap even with the cardboard strip. Tape the ends of the cardboard together on the outside. Apply glue to the long edges of the giftwrap and fold them over the edges of the strip.

13. Glue the insert firmly into the lower part of the box.

14. See if the lid fits on the box. Remove the lid again and let the lid and the box dry separately.

Florentine Box

The picture shows a type of box called Florentine. It can be seen everywhere in boutiques in northern Italy, handsomely decorated with various papers. Since it is an ornamental box and a relatively easy one to make, it is the first one for which patterns are supplied.

As seen in the photo, the lid comes far down over the bottom, differing in this respect from the series of pictures we have just seen. This kind of box has no insert and is thus easier to put together than the other right-angled types.

The assembly procedure is covered by photos 3 through 8 out of the preceding series.

Florentine Box

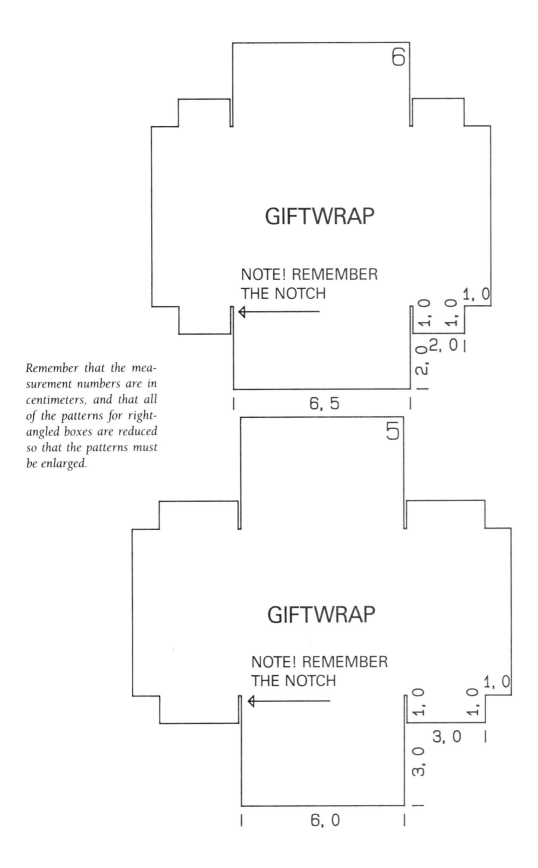

GIFTWRAP

NOTE! REMEMBER
THE NOTCH

1, 0

1, 0 1, 0

2, 0

2, 0

6, 5

*Remember that the mea-
surement numbers are in
centimeters, and that all
of the patterns for right-
angled boxes are reduced
so that the patterns must
be enlarged.*

GIFTWRAP

NOTE! REMEMBER
THE NOTCH

1, 0

1, 0 1, 0

3, 0

3, 0

6, 0

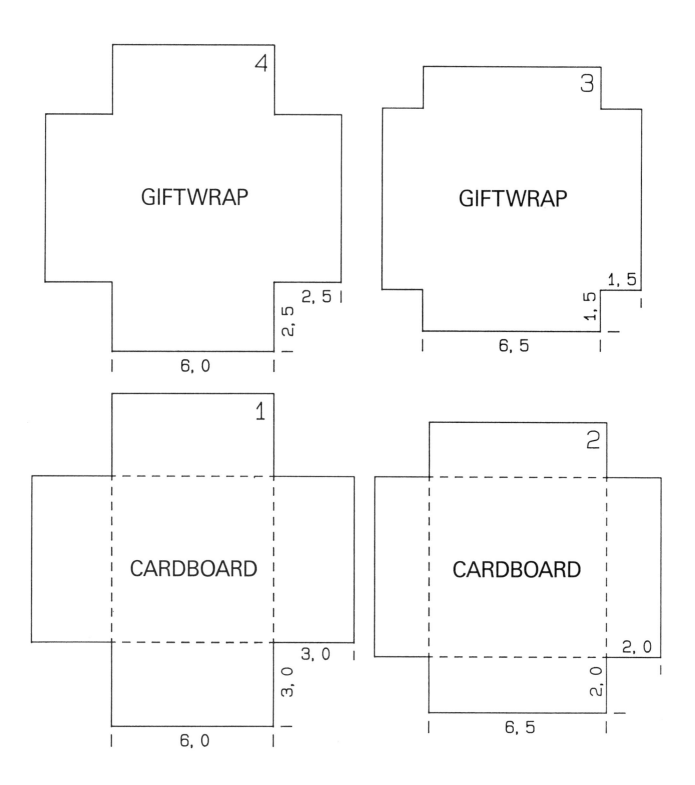

Square Box

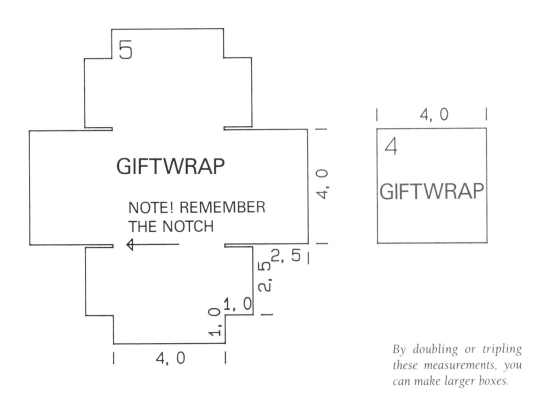

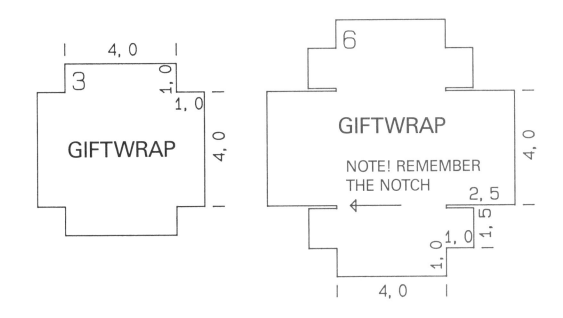

By doubling or tripling these measurements, you can make larger boxes.

Square Box, *continued*

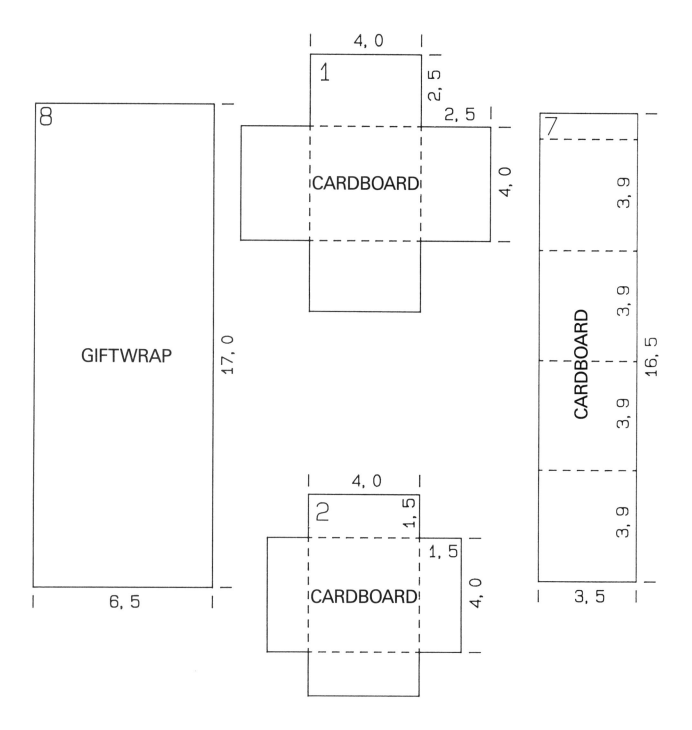

8 — GIFTWRAP — 17, 0 — 6, 5

1 — CARDBOARD — 4, 0 — 2, 5 — 2, 5 — 4, 0

2 — CARDBOARD — 4, 0 — 1, 5 — 1, 5 — 4, 0

7 — CARDBOARD — 3, 9 — 3, 9 — 3, 9 — 3, 9 — 3, 9 — 16, 5 — 3, 5

Oblong Box

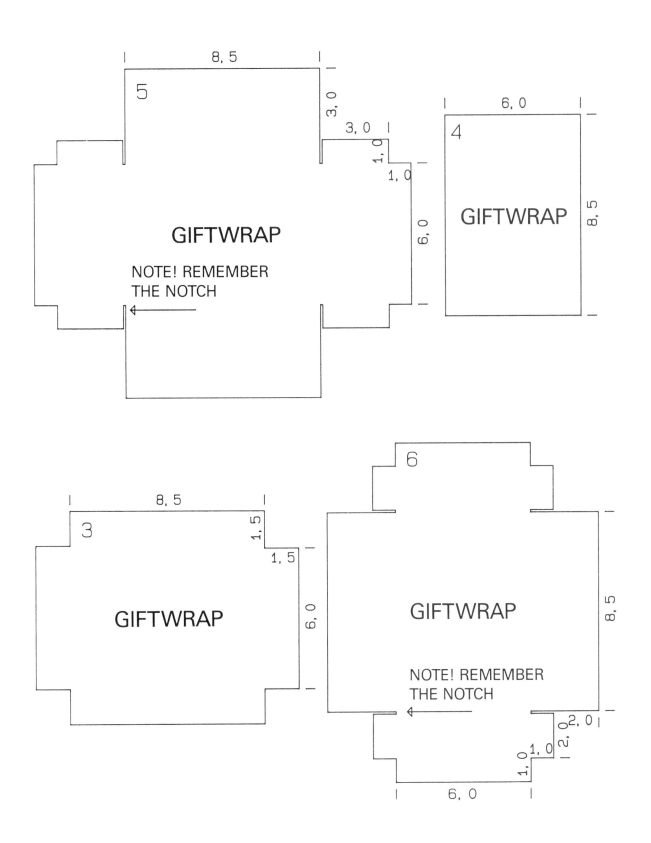

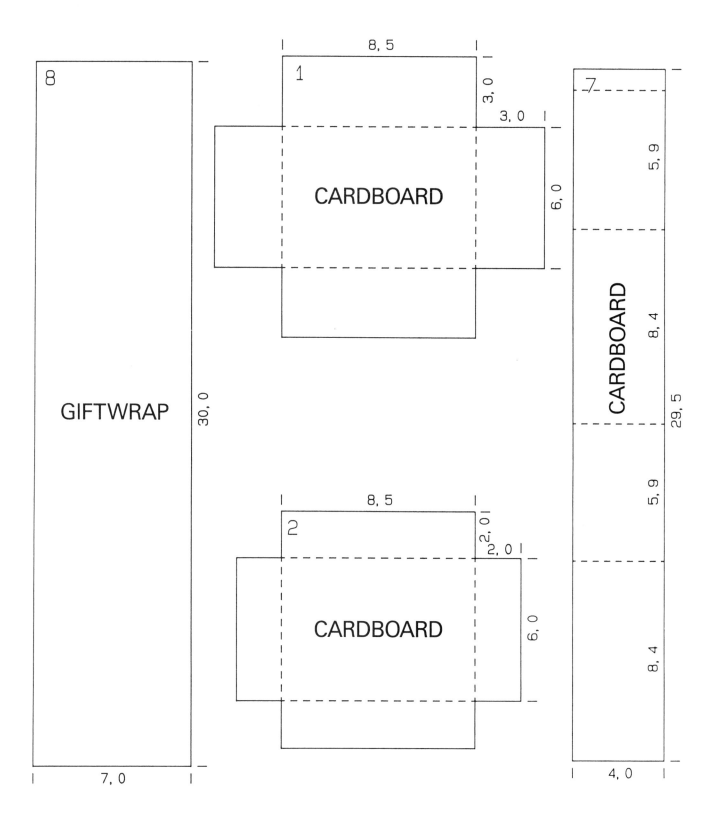

8, 5

1

3, 0

3, 0

CARDBOARD

6, 0

8

GIFTWRAP

30, 0

7

5, 9

CARDBOARD

8, 4

29, 5

5, 9

8, 4

8, 5

2

2, 0

2, 0

CARDBOARD

6, 0

7, 0

4, 0

Long Box ("Pencil Box")

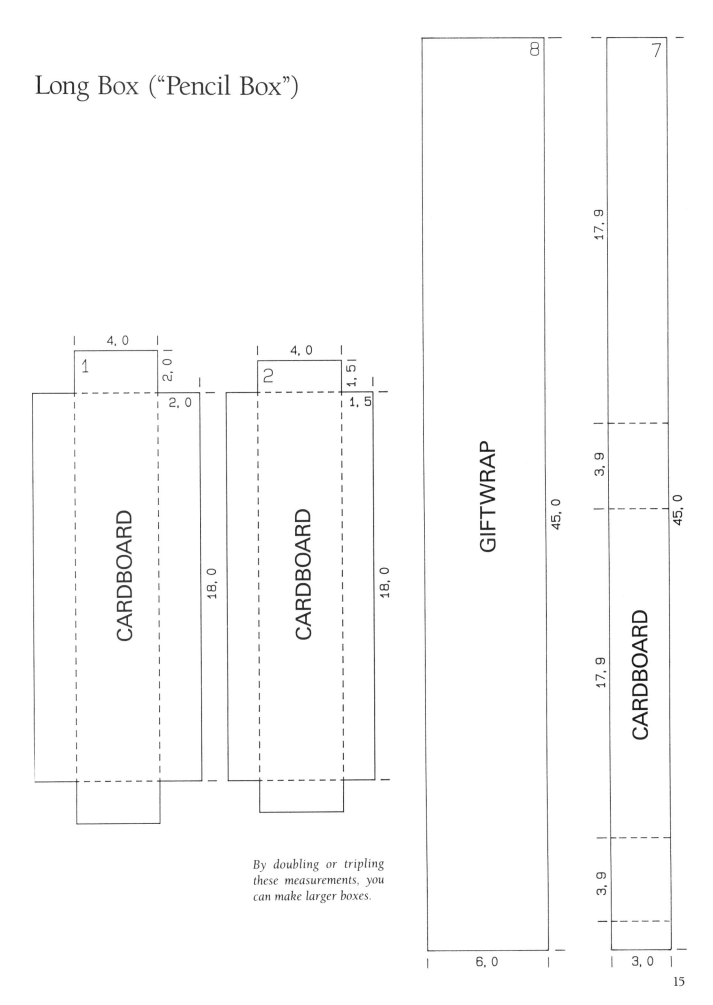

By doubling or tripling these measurements, you can make larger boxes.

15

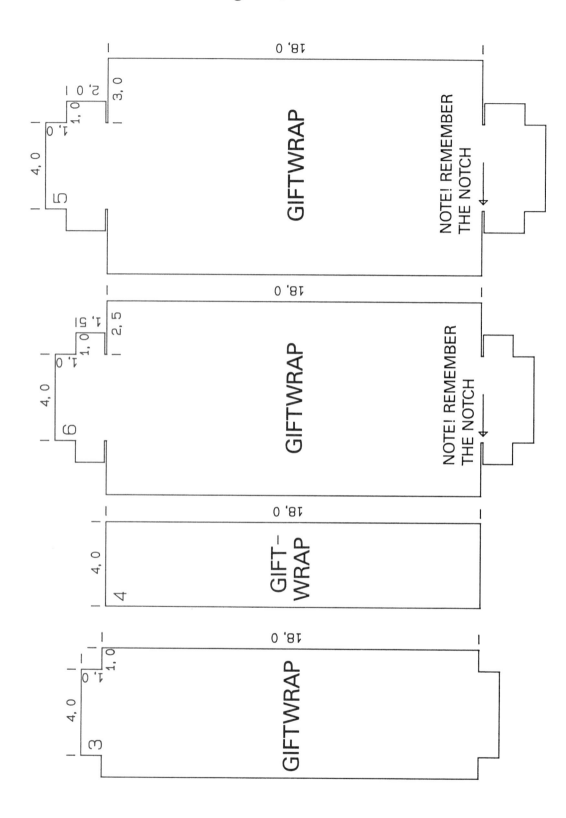

Triangular Box

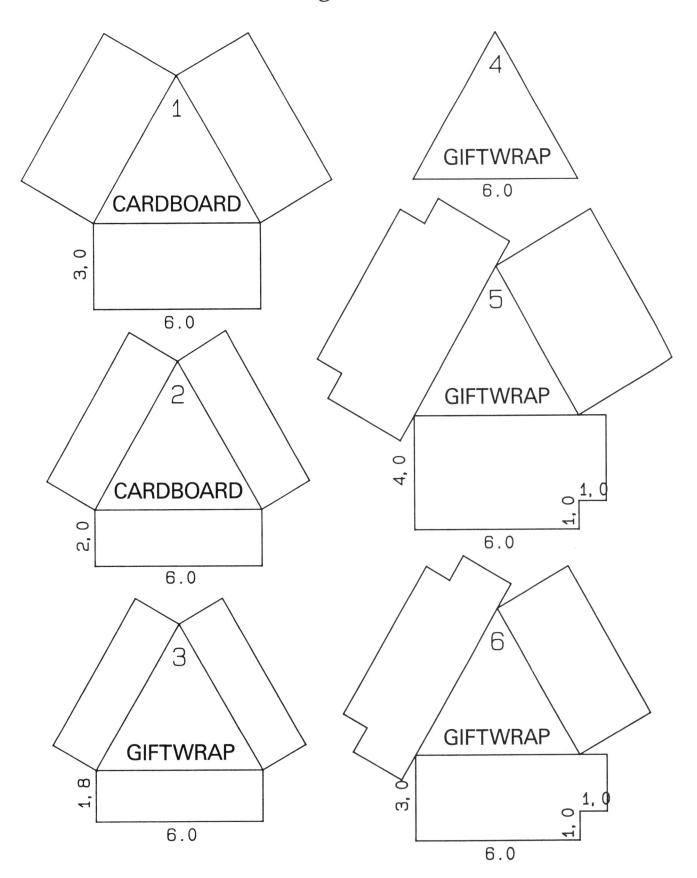

1 CARDBOARD 3,0 6.0

2 CARDBOARD 2,0 6.0

3 GIFTWRAP 1,8 6.0

4 GIFTWRAP 6.0

5 GIFTWRAP 4,0 1,0 1,0 6.0

6 GIFTWRAP 3,0 1,0 1,0 6.0

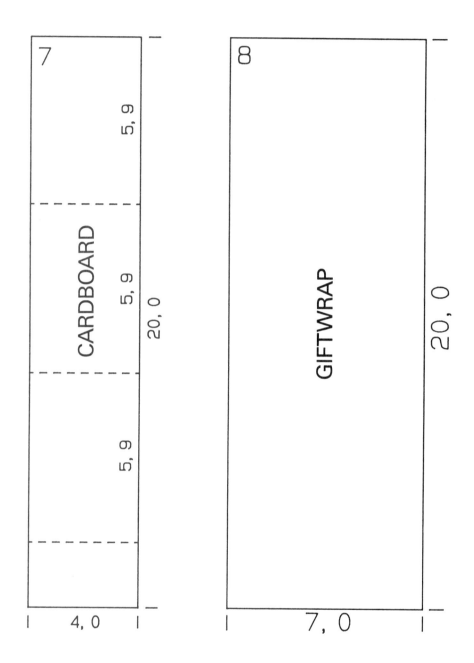

7 CARDBOARD

5, 9

5, 9

5, 9

20, 0

4, 0

8 GIFTWRAP

20, 0

7, 0

Pentagonal Box

Construction of a regular pentagon.

First draw a circle with a compass. Then draw two lines forming right angles at the center of the circle.

Divide in half the line from the center to B.

Put one point of the compass on E and draw an arc from D down to the line between the center and A.

Set the compass points to equal the distance between D and F; put the point on D and draw an arc intersecting the circumference near A. Continue around the circle: with the point on your latest intersection each time, draw three more arcs. Connect the circumference intersections with straight lines inside the circle, and you have your pentagon.

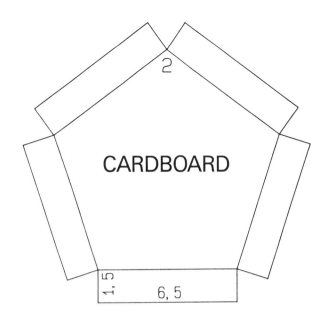

CARDBOARD

2

1, 5   6, 5

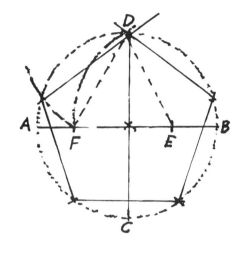

GIFTWRAP

3

1, 0   6, 5

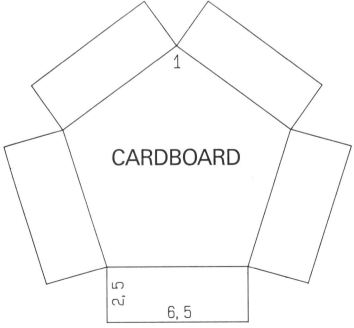

CARDBOARD

1

2, 5   6, 5

GIFTWRAP

4

6, 5

Pentagonal Box, *continued*

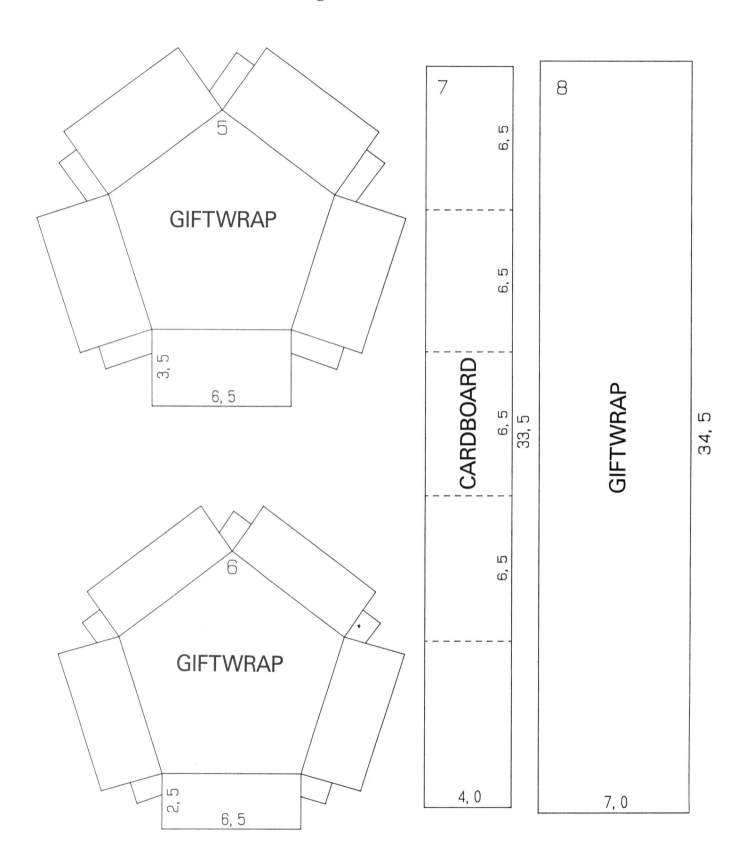

20

Round and Oval Boxes

As will be seen in the instructions on the following pages, the construction of round and oval boxes differs significantly from that of right-angled boxes.

The procedure is completely different and, inasmuch as it is difficult to design an oval box (and the heart-shaped boxes later in the book) on your own, I have thought it best to present the shaped patterns for these at actual size. The long strips still need to be enlarged.

With a piece of carbon paper or merely a piece of ordinary wax paper, you can copy the shapes and transfer them directly to your own cardboard and giftwrap paper.

Making Rounded Boxes

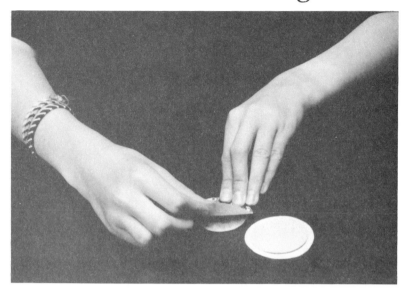

1. *This series of photos, which refers to the patterns on pages 27–30, specifically shows the construction of a round box, but the instructions can also be used for oval boxes (either rounded or pointed) and, with the additional comments on page 26, for heart-shaped boxes as well. Begin with two cardboard pieces of the same shape made with the appropriate form of pattern 8. Apply glue to them and paste a piece of giftwrap (pattern 9) onto each cardboard piece.*

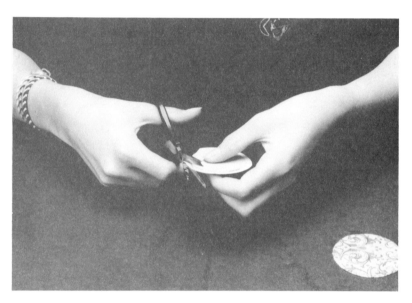

2. *Trim the excess giftwrap.*

3. *Soften all the long strips so they can acquire the necessary curvature. This is done by rolling them between your thumb and index finger in toward yourself. If this is too complicated, they can be bent over the edge of a table.*

4. Take the rounded cardboard strip corresponding to pattern 2 and glue the piece of giftwrap corresponding to pattern 4 to the inner side of the cardboard.

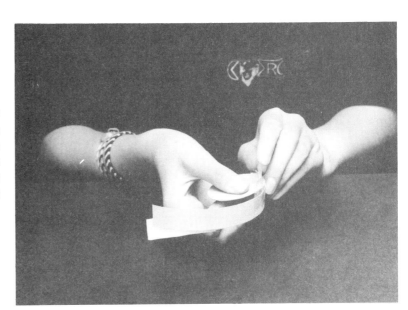

5. Join the piece with tape to one of the pattern-8 pieces (place the side with giftwrap inside). The tape should be placed firmly all the way around. Cut off the excess cardboard and tape the ends together. Do the same with the other pattern-8 piece and the long piece of cardboard corresponding to pattern 1 (which is not covered with giftwrap).

6. Glue the pieces of giftwrap corresponding to patterns 5 and 6 around the bottom and the lid, respectively. The giftwrap should be placed so that it extends far beyond the cardboard on both sides.

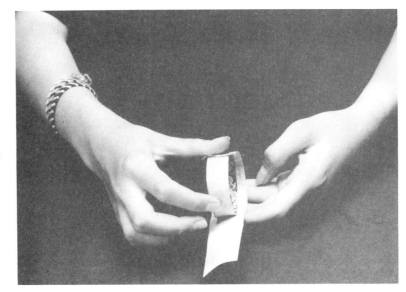

7. Cut small notches into the giftpaper that extends beyond the cardboard, and paste it down inside the box and on the surface of the bottom-piece, respectively.

8. Paste the last two pieces of pattern-9 giftwrap to the pattern-8 pieces and trim the excess paper.

9. Take the widest of the long giftwrap pieces (pattern 7) and draw a line dividing it into one 3-cm strip and one 4-cm strip. Cut them apart and paste the larger one inside the cardboard piece corresponding to pattern 3. Test to see if the insert fits within the bottom-piece. Also remember to test whether the lid fits.

24

10.   Glue the other strip around the insert. Allow 1 cm to extend beyond the edge.

11.   Glue the insert into the bottom.

12.   Cut small notches into the giftwrap (as in photo 7) and fold them down into the box. Remember to let the lid dry separately.

Heart-Shaped Box

The assembly of heart-shaped boxes differs slightly from that of the other shapes.

In contrast to the round and oval boxes, for the heart-shaped box a point must be made in the middle of the otherwise rounded form.

After rounding the strips in your hand or over the edge of a table, you should bend them in the center. This bend becomes the top point of the heart.

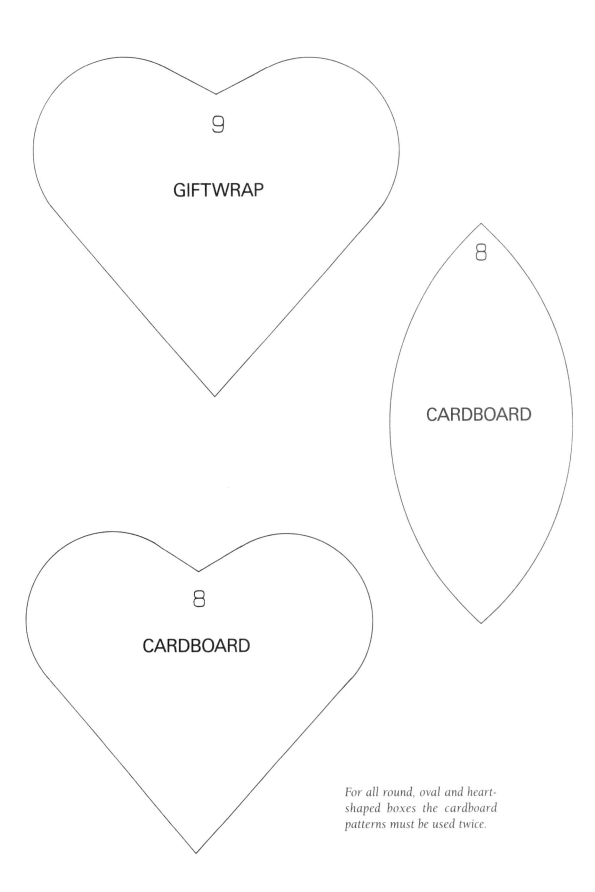

9

GIFTWRAP

8

CARDBOARD

8

CARDBOARD

For all round, oval and heart-shaped boxes the cardboard patterns must be used twice.

Patterns for oval and round boxes.

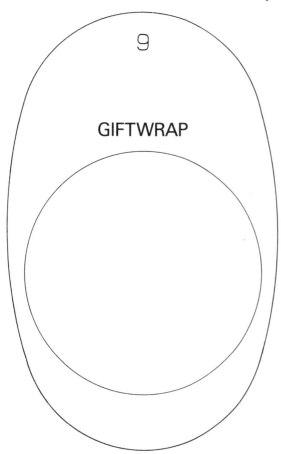

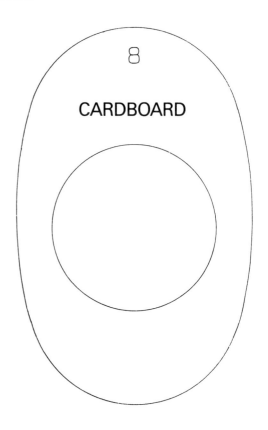

All the patterns on pages 27 and 28 are in the ratio 1:1. The round box, however, can also be made with a radius of (for instance) 4.5 cm (for the cardboard) and 5.5 cm (for the giftwrap), but you would also need to lengthen the strips. Use an ordinary compass to draw the patterns.

The pattern for the giftwrap is to be used four times.

1	2	3	4
CARDBOARD	CARDBOARD	CARDBOARD	GIFTWRAP
28 x 3 cm	28 x 2 cm	28 x 4 cm	29 x 2 cm

5

GIFTWRAP

29 x 5 cm

6

GIFTWRAP

29 x 4 cm

7

GIFTWRAP

29 x 7 cm